D1145981

This b

GREAT
LOST
ALBUMS

GREAT
LOST
ALBUMS

Mark Billingham
David Quantick
Stav Sherez
Martyn Waites

sphere

SPHERE

First published in Great Britain in 2014 by Sphere

Copyright © Mark Billingham Ltd., David Quantick,
Stav Sherez, Martyn Waites 2014

The moral right of the author has been asserted.

A CIP catalogue record for this book
is available from the British Library.

ISBN 978-0-7515-5706-0

Typeset in Sabon by M Rules
Printed and bound in Great Britain by
Clays Ltd, St Ives plc

Papers used by Sphere are from well-managed forests
and other responsible sources.

MIX
Paper from
responsible sources
FSC
www.fsc.org
FSC® C104740

Contents

KYLIE, KANT AND
A KRAFTWERK KRISTMAS

BEELZEBUB, BINGO AND
BOLLOCKS IN A BUCKET

MAD DOGS, MEAT ABUSE AND MUSICALS IN MACCLESFIELD

Foreword

Fickle mistress, Dame Pop. Outside the lucky few, whose warm personalities, glittering talent, wit and generosity of spirit – Gary Barlow, Van Morrison, Count Grishnakh of Death Metal faves Burzum and so on – have made them 'National Treasures', there are many who never quite hit the heights in this crazy business we call 'show'. Furthermore, even for the most stellar of stars, there can be the false move, the misstep, the much-rumoured-but-never-released skeleton in the back catalogue. Many's the time late at night that I've heard the talk turn amongst the cognoscenti to Kraftwerk's lost Christmas album, Dylan's collaboration with Liberace and Morrissey's misguided foray into Panto, the lost prog classic *Dodecahedron* and the Who's first rock opera about a deaf, dumb and blind bingo caller. Enquire within on these and other matters. You will not be disappointed.

Brilliance in one's field is no guarantee of 'celebrity'. Have you ever seen Steve Reich on Celebrity *Pointless*? Sir Peter aka 'Maxwell' Davies on *Chatty Man*? Did Sun Ra ever appear on *Wogan*? Well, yes, to be strictly accurate he did. But the show was never broadcast. Why? Perhaps we shall never know. But I think you take my point. History is told by the victors, they say, and whilst the record review pages of *Take a Break* magazine are filled with today's ephemeral popinjays – Lady Gaga, Muse or Katy Perry, the transvestite ceramicist of 'I Kilned A Girl' fame – truer, rarer, richer talents gather dust in the 'Where Are They Now?' file. Their albums are scattered to the Sue Ryders and Cancer Research shops of the world, where they languish behind old Car Maintenance manuals for Vauxhall Cavaliers, and Frustration with The Popomatic Dice (*Dice missing, will accept 50p*).

Nick 'Charlie' Drake, Vashti 'Mind My' Bunions, The Chive Scissors, Skiffle Widow, The New Potatoes. Names now as forgotten as ACDO, Olga Korbut, Lenny The Lion and the former Yugoslavia. But only fate, perversity and those incompetent stoners in the record company PR departments denied them the fame and riches they deserved. You don't understand. They coulda had class. They could have been contenders. They could have been somebody, instead of bums with one-way tickets to Palookaville, which is what they are, let's face it, Charley.

Sorry, where was I? Oh, yes, the book. The names in this book are well-known. But the albums are not. Alongside their creators' more famous works, the 'Thrillers', the 'Like A Virgins', the 'Tommys', these are the ones that got away. The dwarf idiot half-brothers, the Mushroom Omelette at the end of the Indian menu of rock history.

These days I have to confess that I have little time for rock scholarship. I rarely, if ever, dip into the pages of *Crazy Disc*, *Fab 2001* or *Jazz Magazine*, not even my old alma mater *NME*. These days I'm happy to be 'out of the loops' (dread phrase!) and prefer to have *The Tatler* and *Culottes Ahoy!* 'biked round' to the old pile. It comes to us all in the end, even those fabled firebrands of our youths. Julie Burchill now lives in Penge with her cat Bakunin. Nick Kent runs a candle-making workshop in the New Forest. Tony Parsons is widely tipped to be the next Archbishop of Canterbury.

But when my dear, dear old friends Dennis Quantock and Mike Billingham [*check spellings*], Steve Sherez and Martina White asked me to write a few paid words of introduction to this marvellously slight and affordable volume, how could I resist? These days I tend to spend my time down at the harbour with my nets and lures whistling the odd chorus of nothing more lusty than 'Bobby Shaftoe'. But within these pages are albums for which even I am wide-eyed with anticipation. And, gentle reader, I have lived. Never mind 'attack ships on fire off the shoulder of Orion'. I have seen Shaun Ryder in his underwear backstage at the Northampton Roadmenders Club. I have been around the ring. I have supped long of music's intoxicating draughts.

Think of this book, if you will, as a fusty and mildewed old second-hand shop glimpsed down a back street in a lonely East Anglian seaside village out of season, one such as you might find in the stories of M. R.

James or Robert Aickmann. You slip in, and the little bell jingles, bringing a small hooded man out from the back room. Worryingly he keeps his back to you throughout the conversation, but, in a croaky mumble, he suggests you take a look inside the suitcase by the suit of armour before disappearing into the back room. In the afore-mentioned case, you see treasures that fill your heart with greed and a perverse kind of lust. A first edition of H. P. Lovecraft, a letter signed by Conan Doyle, a framed mezzotint of Dumpy's Rusty Nuts.

One item more than any other makes you catch your breath. Pushing aside a cobwebby curtain that brushes unpleasantly against your cheek, you enter the rear chamber. It is dark and fetid, with a rank sweet odour. 'How much for this 7-inch of "Boys Keep Swinging" on yellow vinyl?' you blurt out, but before you can haggle or speak further, the hooded figure emerges from the shadows with an inhuman gurgle, throws back his hood and reveals himself. It's Jimmy Tarbuck.

No, no, it isn't. Damn this new medication. Perhaps it's the dosage. And don't think of this book like that at all. Think of it as a book full of great lost albums. That is, after all the title, and we should respect it.

This book, then, is for those devoted souls who take popular music seriously, not those shallow individuals who regard music as just an ace way of getting off with girls, dancing till the small hours or generally having an ace time with. No, it is more than this. It is about collecting and cataloguing. It is about reducing a glorious thing of joy to an arid and pointless game of naysaying and nitpicking for sexually inadequate middle-aged men. It is about raising your voice slightly in the pub and putting down that pretty girl who just said she 'quite liked' Gary Numan with a sneery 'Perhaps you should check out the first Neu! album and Kratftwerk's early stuff with Connie Plank! Gary certainly did!' in a plonkingly loud voice.

Yes, that's the real spirit of pop expertise. And this book will help you become the right kind of pop fan; opinionated, hectoring, and able to get through an entire edition of *Later with Jools Holland* without running from the room screaming, 'For Christ sake, take that kora off Damon Albarn and put some Sheila B Devotion on!'

Venceremos!! Enjoy!! Woot!! Get In!!

Stuart Maconie
Montevideo
Summer 2014

PUPPETS, PUNK

AND

PANTOMIME

SMITHS

THE
IKEA SESSIONS

COLDPLAY

RECORDED: 2003
PRODUCER: ALLEN KEY
LABEL: IKEA ENTERTAINMENT

It is a truth universally acknowledged that IKEA make furniture for people who believe they're getting edgy, contemporary, stylish design, but in actual fact have no idea whether what they're sitting on or eating off is good or bad. People who probably don't like it much anyway, and don't really care. So who better than Coldplay to become the furniture giant's band in residence?

'Designed by committee, machine-made, mass-produced and bland,' said Thor Olafson, IKEA UK's Head of Creative Blue Sky Out Of The Box Thinking. 'That's their music. Just like our furniture. That's why we approached them. And because Keane were busy.'

In 2003, Coldplay were on the way up. Their first album, 2000's *Parachutes*, had introduced Chris Martin's privileged whine to the world, given middle managers and sales executives something to listen to in their company cars and, most crucially, provided people in the home counties with aural wallpaper for their dinner parties. 'As soon as we heard "Yellow", we knew that IKEA and Coldplay were meant to go together,' said Olafson. 'Like gin and tonic. Or gravadlax and dill. Or BBC4 and another one of those Nordic Noir series where people in knitwear frown at grey landscapes or stand in cellars with a torch.'

With IKEA's flagship store set to open in Croydon later that year, Olafson approached Coldplay with a radical idea. 'Play your songs in our store,' he said. 'That way people will get to hear what their furniture will sound like in their own homes. We will say: come, sit on our modular KIVIK sofa. Share your long, brooding, evening silences with us. Stare at the TV on the ORRBURG. Ask what time *EastEnders* is on. Profess your love of Ant and Dec. Sigh a lot. Cry, even.'

The crowds flocked. Coldplay set up their instruments, playing live while customers did the famous IKEA shuffle. The resulting album was planned as a giveaway with in-store purchases of over five hundred pounds, provided the customer took home delivery.* Heard now, the songs make

---

* This offer was not valid when buying five hundred pounds' worth of Dime bars or frozen meatballs, but did include IKEA's own-brand coffee because they had to shift it somehow.

for curious listening. Stripped of their customary backing tracks, the instrumentation sounds as weak as Martin's trademark tremulous, over-sensitive yodel, while 'Fix You (But There's Always a Couple of Bits Missing)' loses whatever plaintive longing it may have once had when Mr and Mrs Prebble from Tulse Hill begin arguing over the length of an INGATORP dining room table just before the bridge.

Meanwhile, the band's influence didn't stop on the shop floor. Gwyneth Paltrow, Martin's curvaceous, unpretentious and always up-for-a-laugh wife, brought her love of health foods to bear in the café. Out went IKEA's signature – and hugely popular – meatballs in favour of a range of vegan snacks based on the punishment regime given to chatty monks in the dungeons of a fifteenth-century Trappist monastery. The meals now consisted of artisan unmilled seed bread, water, grass, and an unwashed carrot chopped into 361 pieces. Paltrow considered them a huge success, but customers were unconvinced, choosing to starve instead. She did, however, have concerns that her three children, Apple, Kumquat and Guava, were being inexplicably bullied in the crèche and left the project early.

The sessions came to an abrupt halt soon after that. 'We thought it would be because of artistic differences,' said Olafson, 'but it was nothing like that. Gwyneth wanted to design her own range of healthy, posture-improving furniture (the TALKEMADA range) based on torture implements of the Spanish Inquisition. We couldn't allow our company to be linked with a fascist organisation. Not after the last time.'

So Coldplay departed and Croydon instantly became slightly more interesting. But something of their experience remained. 'I went to see them on their last tour,' said Olafson, 'And when Chris Martin was seated at the piano, I'm sure he was sitting on a KARLSKRONA.'

However, they had left something of themselves behind. Martin, in his haste to leave, took with him three random strangers – two from kitchen fittings and another who'd popped in to buy a couple of BENNOs – believing them to be the other three mute, anonymous members of his band. To this day the plaintive cries of 'Chris, wait for us ... How do we get out?' can be heard echoing round the maze-like walls of the store. The three people he took with him have subsequently gone on to become stadium rockstars.

And no one has noticed.

1. In My Place
   (There's a Lovely HEMNES Shelving System)

2. Clocks (Are Available in the Marketplace and
   They're Very Reasonably Priced)

3. Fix You
   (But There's Always a Couple of Bits Missing)

4. Conscious Uncoupling (See Leaflet for Details)

5. A Rush of Blood to the Head
   (Tripping Over The Kids' DUKTIG)

6. The Scientist (Who Designed the METOD
   MAXIMERA Kitchen System Is a Genius)

7. God Put a Smile upon Your Face
   (When You Sit in a POANG)

8. Death and All His Friends (Shop Here)

9. 42 (Times I've Been round This Store and I Still
   Can't Find the Way Out)

10. Cemeteries of London
    (Tottenham, Croydon, Lakeside, Wembley)

ANGEL'S
DELIGHT

BY

JAMES BROWN

RECORDED: 1988
PRODUCER: JAMES BROWN
LABEL: PHENCYCLIDINE

In 1988 James Brown, the Godfather of Soul, the Minister of Super Heavy Funk, Soul Brother Number One, the Uncle of Funkle, the Rajah of Rhythm, the Akond of Swank, was having a few personal problems. He'd fallen out with so many former collaborators that he was reduced to fining himself. His hit career had dried up (the follow up to *Living in America*, the somewhat derivative *Still Living in America*, hadn't even made the charts), and while every act from Public Enemy to Terry Wogan was sampling his beats, James Brown literally could not get arrested. Except in the non-literal sense of literally, that is, because on 17 July , in Aiken County, South Carolina, he was arrested in the literal sense of literally, for possession of angel dust and wonky hair.

Wonky hair, in and of itself, is not a problem, but angel dust is a very different kettle of piranha fish. Highly addictive, with a powerful 'rush', once the initial funny fizzy sensation in the mouth has worn off, angel dust can make the user became mentally unstable while possessed of the strength of ten men. Now, imagine that strength and mental instability in the hands of a frankly already part-bonkers soul legend and what you – or rather, the Aiken County Police department – had on their hands was a cross between Sly Stone on a bad day and the Incredible Hulk on a very bad day.

Brown resisted arrest, resisted argument, resisted logic and resisted the UK changeover from the imperial to the metric system. He was finally restrained when an officer showed him a mirror and Brown, recognising an equal, calmed down long enough to be placed in a cell. Even then he managed to somehow eat his bed and organise a cockroach rebel army before he passed out in a pool of his own funk.

The next day in court, Brown was repentant and shame-faced. He promised never to do it again. 'Say it loud,' he said, 'I'm ashamed and proud.' When it was pointed out to him that you can't be ashamed and proud at the same time, James Brown amended his statement to, 'Say it loud, I'm not proud and I'm proud.' The judge agreed with the DA that this was probably the best they were going to get, and sentenced Brown to eighty minutes of community service in the form of a new album, whose profits would go to the Aiken County Youth Services Combined Marching Band and Gymnastics Team.

Brown readily agreed and summoned his touring band by climbing to the roof of the courthouse and shining an Afro-shaped beacon into the night sky. Unfortunately, on the way to the studio he ran into his old dealer, Huggy 'Terrifying' Bear, who promptly sold him a pound of the legendary 'Gabriel' dust. The resulting recording session, in which ten engineers were wounded and Vanilla Ice was accidentally inhaled by a hippo, was generally agreed by the survivors to be 'the funkiest thing since the atom bomb'. Unfortunately, someone managed to chop up the tapes and snort them, so all that remains is this tantalising if bizarre track listing.

1. Don't Make Me Funky
   (You Wouldn't Like Me When I'm Funky)

2. Spoken Interlude
   (Lizards Are Coming)

3. I Feel Good ... Wait ... I Feel Amazing ... Wait ... I
   Don't Feel Very Well

4. Get On Up I Feel Like Being a Washing Machine

5. Spoken Interlude 2
   (More Lizards Are Coming)

6. It's a Man's Man's Man's Man's Man's Man's
   Man's Man's Man's Man's Man's Man's Man's Man's
   I'm a Warthog Man's Man's Man's Man's Man's
   Man's World

7. Papa's Got a Brand-New What Is That Oh God It's
   Got Wings It's Got Claws It's Not a Lizard It's a
   Dragon AAAAAARGH!

8. Spoken Interlude 3
   (Living with Our Dragon Masters)

THE
COMMON ROOM

BY

MUMFORD & SONS

RECORDED: 2004
PRODUCER: MARCUS MUMFORD/BEN LOVETT/
MR JACKSON THE MUSIC TEACHER
LABEL: TRUST FUND RECORDS

'As good as anything they've ever done.'
'You won't hear a better album by Mumford & Sons.'
'Every bit as talented then as they are now!'

These are just some of the reviews from people privileged enough to have heard *The Common Room*, an album recorded by Marcus Mumford and his school chum Ben Lovett when they were just sixteen. Admittedly, these are people who hate everything the band has ever done, but still …

Marcus Oliver Johnstone Mumford and Benjamin Lovett had bonded, aged only eleven, over a shared love

MUMFORD & SONS 13

of fine tawny port and the comedy stylings of Cornish funnyman Jethro. Progressing through the years at St Mimsy's College (£45,000 per term), they quickly became accomplished musicians and songwriters, while maintaining exemplary standards in all their academic subjects and memberships of the Debating Society, First XI and Combined Cadet Force. By the time they reached the lower sixth, Mumford and Lovett, despite being tipped for jobs in the intelligence services and the City respectively, had decided on a career in music.

'It was in our blood,' Mumford said years later. 'We'd been heavily influenced by so many amazing artists. Enya was one ... and Tanita Tikaram was the other one. Sting's lute experiments also left their mark on both of us.' It was not the only thing to leave its mark during their years at King's, and some of their less happy experiences were chronicled on *The Common Room*, in songs such as 'Thank You Sir, May I Have Another' and most notably 'Matron, That Stings': *Your chubby nursemaid fingers/Marking me for weeks/Like common sausages/Red against my teenage cheeks.*

Armed with only a vintage Gibson acoustic guitar and a handmade tea-chest from Fortnum & Mason, Mumford and Lovett set out to record a series of songs shot through with the rebellion so typical of most boys their age. 'We were sick to the stomach of all the privilege we had,' Lovett told *Horse & Hound* in 2012. 'We were stifled by it, crushed by the weight of it day after bloody day. We were grateful for the nice equipment, mind you.'

Using every spare minute and study break, the boys began laying down tracks in the sixth form common room that would give their debut its title. They dug deep into the well of personal experience, producing songs that railed against their lives of extraordinary luxury, yet also celebrated their religious faith and an Englishness that had perhaps been neglected for far too long. 'Yeah, we really loved the English countryside,' said Mumford. 'Especially those sizeable bits of it our fathers owned.'

Mocked by their peers – who gleefully christened them Bumfuck & Sons – the duo found themselves in a creative impasse midway through the Michaelmas term (somewhere between double Latin and Wednesday Games). In an effort to recharge their artistic batteries, they packed their Boden haversacks and decamped to the Left Bank in Paris, intending to feed from the intense and heady experience of painters and poets, bohemians and *clochards*. The plan was admirable, but flawed. They had intended to sleep rough, but after a single horrendous afternoon, during which Mumford was sold a stale baguette and Lovett felt a bit chilly, they both made frantic phone calls home and spent the rest of the trip in the George V.

Of course, to those who enjoy feasting on the rich fare of *Sigh No More* and *Babel*, this adolescent effort will be no more than thin gruel. But it's a worthwhile snack. Were it not for this early experiment, and the duo's subsequent exposure to real country and folk courtesy of Garth Brooks and Billy Ray Cyrus, those later masterpieces might never have been made at all.

1. I Ain't Nobody's Fag

2. I Won't Bend Down

3. England, My Garden of Delights
   (Most of Surrey and a Good Chunk of Kent)

4. Matron, That Stings

5. Forgotten Kit (Wear Your Pants)

6. Thank You, Sir, May I Have Another

7. Giving My Fucking Allowance Away to the Poor
   (Well, Thinking about It)

8. Carpentry Was Good Enough for Jesus
   (A* in Woodwork)

9. Awake My Soul, It's Time for Rowing Practice

FRANKLY
WIDOW TWANKLY

BY
MORRISSEY

RECORDED: 1999
PRODUCER: BOZ BOORER/CHRISTOPHER BIGGINS
LABEL: PARLOPHONE

Morrissey has previous when it comes to recording material and not releasing it. He ditched an entire album in 1993, confining himself to bed for three months after Alan Bennett walked by on the other side of the street without waving. He later recorded tracks with Tony Visconti, then refused to release them after witnessing Visconti looking into a butcher's shop window and later sneaking back to buy a bag of pork scratchings. But without doubt it is *Frankly Widow Twankly*, his great lost panto album, that has invited most speculation.

'There's nothing as British as panto,' Morrissey

declared. When the interviewer pointed out that panto was essentially a bastardisation of the Italian *commedia dell'arte*, Morrissey spanked him with a wet slipper. Carrying on regardless, thus was born *Frankly Widow Twankly*. (Incidentally, when the same interviewer pointed out that it should be 'Twanky' not 'Twankly', Morrissey said it rhymed, so it was correct and not to challenge him. He then went back to working on lyrics claiming all British monarchs were descended from Oliver Cromwell.)

Morrissey set to work, gathering a crack team of seasoned panto session musicians around him. At first he objected to the smell of Old Holborn pipe tobacco and the sight of *Angler's Monthly* and *Practical Caravanner* in the studio, but he was informed by co-producer Biggins (famous for his work with cheeky scouse sex-bomb Cilla Black) that it was a different way of working; a different culture. Morrissey, unhappy – always, always unhappy – grudgingly went along with it.

He also surrounded himself with the very best talent to realise his artistic vision. The Krankies were called in to play the comedy Chinese policemen double act, here called 'Meat' and 'Murder'. A heavily refreshed Charles Hawtrey played the part of the Genie of the Lamp; in a spirit of reconciliation Mike Joyce featured as Baron Hardup; Judge John Weeks was the Sheriff of Nottingham and John Barrowman was on hand to give Mozza his Dick.* David

* Dick as in Dick Whittington. Give as in perform the role. God, you people!

Bowie (at his most chameleon-like) was scheduled to appear as the Thin White Dame, but soon left after an argument with Morrissey because of his insistence on bringing his own Bovril sandwiches to rehearsals. He was replaced by the ever-reliable John Inman. Morrissey now had his dream team around him. 'When I looked at some of the people I was working with,' he said later, 'I just felt my essential Englishness rise up.'

Unfortunately Morrissey and Biggins clashed constantly throughout the sessions,* Morrissey's insistence that only organic lentils could be used during the cake-making scene creating a tense atmosphere. Morrissey then decided to take the production on tour.

It opened at the Pavilion Theatre on Cromer Pier, with Morrissey singing the perennial classic 'Oh I Do Like to Be beside the Seaside' in his own inimitable manner: *Oh I do like to be beside the seaside/But only when it's grim and really bleak/Oh I do like to stroll along the prom, prom, prom/While I pray they drop a nuclear bomb, bomb, bomb*. Then moving on to some traditional call and response with the audience: 'Have you all had a lovely Christmas, boys and girls? Anyone who felt the need to viciously slaughter poultry in order to enjoy themselves can leave now.'

Sadly, it only lasted one performance, as Morrissey, who refused to throw sweets into the audience as they

* Morrissey would later chronicle their fallings-out on his coruscating hit single 'Biggins's Mouth Strikes Again'.

contained gelatine, almost blinded a four-year-old boy by hurling a stick of celery at him. Fearing another court case, Morrissey abandoned the project and fled the country for Jamaica where, rumour has it, he collaborated with Peter Tosh on his great lost reggae album, *Ragga Polari*. But that's another story.*

* Oh no it isn't.

1. The Principal Boy with the Thorn in His Side

2. Meat Is Murder (Even For a Pantomime Cow) (feat. The Krankies)

3. Oh I Do Like to Be beside the Seaside

4. I've Got a Lovely Bunch of Organic Coconuts

5. How Soon is the Interval?

6. Frankly Widow Twankly (feat. John Inman)

7. He's Behind Me, Oh Yes He Is! (feat. John Barrowman)

8. The More You Rub Me the Closer I Get (feat. Charles Hawtrey)

9. Devious Truculent and Unreliable (feat. Judge John Weeks)

10. Babes on Saddleworth Moor

11. There Is a Light That Never Goes Out (Ensemble)

REPULSION (ORIGINAL SOUNDTRACK)

BY

ELVIS PRESLEY

RECORDED: 1965
PRODUCER: COLONEL TOM PARKER
LABEL: UNRELEASED

The mid-1960s were not kind to the King of rock and roll. The British Invasion had conquered the charts, kids were starting to grow their hair, and Elvis Presley was mired in naff-movie soundtrack hell. Alone at Graceland, watching the Beatles on his last unshot TV set, the King desperately yearned to be cool again.

It was on the set of *Maui Cheeseburger* (1965) that Presley told Colonel Tom he was sick of making Hawaiian films and wanted to branch out into something serious. Parker initially managed to defer Elvis with a shiny new belt buckle and a Transit van full of bacon-banana butties, but in the end, the King got his way.

In one of those fortuitous twists of fate that seem written by the gods, Parker met the diminutive Polish director Roman Polanski at a party at Jack Nicholson's place. Colonel Tom, who owned a 50 per cent share of all of Elvis's royalties, immediately saw a way to placate Presley and, at the same time, open him up to a new, more sophisticated fan-base. Buoyed by the critical acclaim for *Knife in the Water*, Polanski was so horrified when he heard Parker's proposition that for the first time in his life he was lost for words. Fortunately, Parker knew the right people and – a large cheque and a clammy handshake later – Elvis was on his way to Swinging London.

On his first day on the set of *Repulsion*, Elvis turned up in a Hawaiian shirt, lei, and Speedos, wanting to know what his part was. Parker quickly led him away and explained that concentrating solely on the music was Elvis's chance to show he was a true artist, a musician's musician. He then promptly ushered him off-set and ordered him to enjoy himself. Presley took in the sights and (mainly) the tastes of Swinging London, eating both Fortnum's and Wimpy out of their entire supplies of peanut butter and ketchup.

A few weeks later and several stone heavier, Elvis turned up at the studios and sat down to watch a rough cut of the film. According to eyewitnesses, the King ate seven cheeseburgers before the credits, held Colonel Tom's hand during the scary bits, and discreetly puked into his popcorn container every time the rabbit appeared. 'What the hell was that?' Elvis asked as the credits rolled, and Parker had to patiently explain the concept of art movies and then, the concept of art. 'Man, all that chick needs to set her straight is some action,' was Elvis's only reply.

The atmosphere during the recordings was tense. Elvis kept calling Polanski *little man* and couldn't understand the director's accent, which led to some inevitable confusion. An early cut of the film with Presley's original soundtrack was found in the janitor's closet of a peep show in Amsterdam by the music journalist Jon Reed. The difference to the later, more minimalist score is astonishing. With a crack team of musicians backing him, Elvis manages to misunderstand every single scene in an almost Derridean act of reading against the grain. When Carol is walking through a predatory London, Elvis sings a jaunty 'I Walk the (Border)Line'; when she lays down terrified in her bed, Elvis drops into *sotto voce* and tenderly whispers, *Pull yourself together, Mama/All you need is a big strapping man*. As hands come out of the walls, Elvis croons, *Uh-huh/Uh-huh/Uh-huh*, to the beat of the emerging limbs. Production was finally stopped after Elvis sang a beautiful version of 'Love Me Tender'. Unfortunately, he was singing it over Carol's rape scene.

Elvis went back to making the kind of films he understood, films such as *A Big Hunk O' Honolulu* (where he finally got to wear the shirt and Speedos combo) while Polanski wiped the entire soundtrack and brought in

Chico Hamilton. Sadly, there was only enough left in the budget to pay for ten minutes of Hamilton's music, which explains why so many scenes from this mesmerising film take place in absolute silence.

1. Are You Paranoid Tonight?

2. Cut Me Tender

3. Always Out of My Mind

4. I Walk the (Border)Line

5. Mystery Stain

6. Mindbreak Motel > Girl Very Unhappy (Medley)

7. She's Not You (And I'm Not Her)

8. Return Her to Sender

9. Aloha in Hawaii

PISTOLS
AT THE PROMS

BY

THE SEX PISTOLS

RECORDED: 2002
PRODUCER: BBC OUTSIDE BROADCAST UNIT
LABEL: BOOTLEG

The lights in the Royal Albert Hall dimmed. The well-dressed audience finished their conversations, put down their rustling programmes, switched off their mobile phones and readied themselves for the performance. The conductor, Vladimir Jurovski, entered. He bowed in polite acknowledgement made his way to the podium, from where he cast his eyes over the London Philharmonic Orchestra. He tapped his baton, waited a few seconds, then raised it ... and the Overture began.

As the music built to a crescendo, a medium-height figure entered from the wings. Looking suave in a tuxedo, he sauntered to the microphone at the centre of the stage and gazed out at the audience. He smiled. 'Ever got the feeling you're in for a jolly good night's entertainment?' he asked, and the audience applauded.

John Lydon had arrived.

The year was 2002 and the BBC wanted to do something special to mark the Queen's Golden Jubilee. 'Wouldn't it be great,' said one perfectly sober exec to another in the Groucho one night, 'to get the Sex Pistols back together for it?'

'We could have them at the proms with the London Philharmonic, or some shit,' said his equally sober friend.

'Brilliant. I'll call Malcolm ...'

After that, it was relatively easy. Calls were placed to every member of the band: John Lydon in LA, Steve Jones in LA, Paul Cook in Bert Greco's Pie and Mash Shop, Bethnal Green – and they were on. The only one who wanted nothing to do with the project was original bassist Glen Matlock. 'Jesus Christ,' he said, 'haven't those arseholes got better things to do?' The answer was no, of course not, which was why they were agreeing to the gig. 'We'll find another bass player,' insisted Lydon, now Britain's premier butter salesman. 'One who doesn't subscribe to the tired clichés the media would want us all to believe, that tries to tell us what's best, that doesn't want us to think for ourselves anymore. I mean not think for ourselves any more. No. Just a minute. Yes. I meant the other way round. I think. Right. Where was I? The media wants us to think for ourselves. No, that's not right either ...'

Rehearsals started in earnest a few days before the concert. Jurovski had briefed the orchestra to expect something raw, visceral – and to let their playing respond in kind. He was in for a shock when the Pistols arrived. 'Glen's not here, so we can do the songs as we originally intended,' said Lydon. 'None of that horrible shouting. Nice and jolly. Here's the lyrics.'

Jurovski stared open-mouthed as he read. *God save the Queen/A smashing human being/Her enemies are raving/She's really good at waving*. It continued: *She puts up with some flack/And she can't answer back/Her son's a proper nutter/Can I tempt you to some butter?*

Jurovski was appalled. 'I thought we'd be working with the last of England's anarchists,' he told a suitably smarmy Huw Edwards. 'Honestly, the orchestra were more punk than they were. Especially the woodwind. But that's not surprising, really, they've always been a bit edgy.'

Things went from bad to worse. *Hedge funds in the UK/We give them our cash/They give us surprisingly good yields*, crooned Lydon, as another famous track was revisited.

When asked why he had changed all the words, the spiky-haired gurner was unapologetic. 'The songs used to represent us when we wrote them ... or when Glen wrote them ... now they represent us as we are. Wanting to smash the system takes it out of one, doesn't it?'

Their replacement bass player turned out to be none other than Paul McCartney. Unfortunately, the former Beatle and sometime Wing had not received the memo. While the rest of the band wore full evening dress, Macca made his entrance, thumbs aloft, wearing a black bin liner with his hair spiked into a mohican. John Lydon just shook his head. Careful listeners might hear him mumbling, 'No bloody class, these Northerners,' as he turned away.

Proceedings were slightly enlivened by the appearance of David Bowie (at his most chameleon-like) who, wearing only a leotard and oversized safety pin, performed a sinuous mime symbolising the spirit of punk. Steve Jones's opinions on both Bowie's performance and sexuality can clearly be heard on the recording, even above the sound of the raging timpani and flugelhorns.

Classical it may have been, but the concert was most certainly not a classic. Lydon kept glancing at his watch as if he had somewhere better to be, while McCartney stood at the back looking embarrassed and repeatedly calling out titles of his own songs in the hope the rest of the band would take the hint and let him play one. Jones barely bothered and Cook kept stopping to check the football scores on his phone. The orchestra, however, played with passion and brio. The audience, more used to typical proms fare, believed they had witnessed a display of cutting-edge rock and roll. They returned to the home counties quite certain they had lived dangerously for the night.

The concert was, of course, a massive sell-out. Mixing-desk recordings of the gig circulated immediately and for a while they were the hottest bootleg property around. Until people listened to the songs.

Punk, it seemed, was well and truly dead.

1. Pretty Vacant Second Homes

2. God Save the Queen!

3. Holidays in the Sun
   (Umbria's Lovely at This Time of Year)

4. (No) Problems

5. Friggin' in the Riggin' (Of My Private Yacht)

6. Hedge Funds in the UK

7. Who Killed Bambi?
   (Outside of Hunting Season)

8. Silly Thing
   (There's *Always* Time for a Glass of Pimm's)

9. Hey Jude

10. God Save the Queen
    (encore: National Anthem)

THE
SATANIC CHORUSES

BY
U2

RECORDED: 2000
PRODUCER: DANIEL LANOIS
LABEL: DEVIL'S ISLAND

U2 had collaborated with everyone from Brian Eno to Salman Rushdie, from Luciano Pavarotti to David Bowie (at his most chameleon-like). They had tried to end poverty, occasionally stopped war, reinvented acid house and made the world aware of the Berlin Wall less than a year after it had come down. So what was left for the 'Asda Joy Division'? After a hastily convened meeting in the bathroom of their new airship, *The Dutch Tax Break*, the band decided that the one thing holding them back was being, as drummer Larry Grayson put it, 'Such good people. I mean it, we've done so much for the world and what has our reward been? Wealth, yeah, and fame, but to what avail? None avail, that's what.'

As they relaxed in individual tubs and lathered themselves, guitarist The Hedge proposed a new plan; as everyone called them hypocrites every time they did anything, maybe they should just stop being nice and enjoy themselves. Bassist Adam Something agreed; they'd been holier than thou, now it was time to be nastier than thou. And lead singer Bongo settled it when he revealed he'd been trying to find out who had all the good tunes and had finally discovered the truth. 'It's the Devil!' he said, to gasps from his band.

And so was recorded one of the lostiest albums of all time. Opening with a moving yet also chilling version of 'Son of My Father' by Kim Jong-un, with the Hedge's trademark dated flange guitar all up it, *The Satanic Choruses* set out its stall on top of some little kiddies' stalls and burned them to the ground. From the horrifying duet 'With Or Without U (Boats)', with its snake-like vocal from Tony Blair and rap by Bonzo (*Hey, Tony, if you please/Where's them Goddam WMDs?/'Cos I've travelled there and back/I can't find them in Iraq/Go on, Tone, give me a clue … am I getting hotter? Colder?*) to the awesome 'Money (I've Not Done Anything Good Since)', in which Martin Amis and Roger Waters bring the house, and indeed everyone else, down, *The Satanic Choruses* is truly *horrible*. Even the normally melodic 'Yesterday', introduced by Bilbo with the words, 'Matt Monroe stole this song from the Beatles and we're stealing it back', is reduced to a kind of human flesh soup by guest vocalist George W. Bush, singing in a weird Texan nasal twang that suggests Dubya's been on a George Jones jag.

Then, in an attempt to follow the success of 'We Are the World', U2 came up with 'We're Not So Bad', with a line each taken by everyone from Vladimir Putin to 'Blakey' from *On the Buses*. *I'm not so bad*, sings Abu Hamza, before trying to hand, or rather hook the mic to Katie Hopkins. *When you get to know me/Maybe you'll want to blow me*, adds Piers Morgan hopefully. *We're not so bad/We're not even mad*, duet John McCririck and Robert Mugabe in sweet, sweet harmony. It's a fitting closer to an album that would have changed U2's career had not manager Paul McGuinness come back from holiday, shouted at Bonio and the boys a lot, and incinerated the master tapes immediately.

1. Son of My Father (feat. Kim Jong-un)

2. Money (Amis and Waters Megamix)

3. With Or Without U (Boats)

4. Monday, Bank Holiday Monday

5. Where the Bank Accounts Have No Name

6. Yesterday (I Made £87,000 in Interest)

7. Tuesday, Pancake Tuesday

8. 11 O'Clock Dick Rock

9. I Still Haven't Found What I'm Hooking For
    (With Abu Hamza)

10. We're Not So Bad

11. Wednesday, Sheffield Wednesday

ALL YOU NEED IS GLOVE: THE BEST OF PUPPET GLAM

BY

VARIOUS ARTISTS

RECORDED: 1974
PRODUCER: MICKEY MOST
LABEL: TRACY ISLAND RECORDS

By the time the seventies were only a few years old, British music had changed beyond recognition. The warty sixties Rock Gods who stank of Watney's Red Barrel and looked like they'd shag your Granny just for a laugh had been replaced. Record buyers and concert goers now worshipped a new breed of pop star; men who wore feather boas, glittery boob-tubes and hats with mirrors on; who blow-dried their hair and slapped on more make-up every morning than Quentin Crisp got through in a month. The Glam-Rockers had taken over.

These early years of the decade were also a Golden Age for puppet-based, televisual entertainment for children. The nation's youngsters could not get enough of small furry bears and squeaky dogs. They flocked to watch the comical adventures of emus, piglets, knitted cats and crudely animated creatures who lived on the moon and may or may not have been mice.*

It took a record producer of rare vision to see that bringing these two pop-culture phenomena together would be creative alchemy of the most innovative kind. And would also make him a small fortune. RAK supremo Mickey Most had made his name working with a number of groundbreaking artists including Herman's Hermits, Smokie and Mary Hopkin. Now, in his boldest move to date, he instigated a project in which the foremost Glam artists of the time would duet on their greatest hits with some of the country's favourite puppets.

What could possibly go wrong?

If Most had thought that pop stars could be difficult to work with, he had reckoned without the madness, ego-mania and substance-abuse that was rife in the closed and mysterious world of the celebrity puppet. Emu had a cocaine habit that even David Bowie found alarming. Basil Brush refused to leave his trailer until Most stopped the wind from blowing and Lamb Chop was wanted for

---

* They're clearly not mice as they live on the moon for God's sake.

murder in twelve American states. It was not all one-way traffic, of course. Slade's Dave Hill immediately fell out with Ollie Beak; Marc Bolan had a minor breakdown, unable to decide if Bagpuss was a bag or a puss; and recording had to be stopped for two days after Gary Glitter got a little over-friendly with Tiny Clanger. The sessions were tricky, to say the least ...

Despite this, the album they produced had magical moments a-plenty. The opening track sees Sweet and Sooty tearing through 'Ballroom Blitz' in fine style, *Are you ready, Steve?/Uh-huh/Andy?/Yeah/Sooty? Sooty ... ??* Cockney Rebel and Basil Brush work wonderfully together, the voices of Harley and Brush as perfectly married as Gram and Emmylou's ever were, and the Clangers' touching version of 'Space Oddity' is lifted to almost mythic heights, thanks to David Bowie (at his most chameleon-like) turning in a masterly performance as the Soup Dragon.

But trouble was just around the corner.

Tingha and Tucker got together with Pinky and Perky to demand a greater royalty for double-acts. They hired a top legal team, brought in Zippy from Rainbow as an enforcer, and Most quickly began to fear that his entire music empire was on the line. The album might still have been released, were it not for an unfortunate incident during filming for the *Old Grey Whistle Test*, when Roxy Music walked out of the studios after Emu bit Eno in the knackers.

A shame, because *All You Need Is Glove* deserves a

listen: for its unlikely yet adorable collaborations, the unheralded guitar talents of the Pipkins' Hartley Hare, and most especially the moment towards the end when you can clearly hear Gary Glitter asking Harry Corbett how old Sooty's girlfriend is.

1. Sooty and Sweet: Ballroom Blitz

2. T-Rex, feat. Bagpuss: Hot Glove

3. David Bowie and the Clangers: Space Oddity

4. Cockney Rebel and Basil Brush: Mr Soft and Plush

5. Roxy Music and Emu: Glove Is the Drug

6. Pinky and Perky and Suzi Quatro: Devil Gate Drive

7. Bungle and Alvin Stardust: My Coo Ca Choo

8. Tinga and Tucker and Slade: Cum On Feel the Fur

9. Gary Glitter and Lamb Chop: Do You Wanna Touch Me? (No, Thank You)

10. Wizzard, feat. Topo Gigio: Angel Fingers Up Your Backside

McWHIRTER'S ORIGINALS

BY

LED ZEPPELIN

RECORDED: 1968
PRODUCER: JIMMY PAGE
LABEL: BOOTLEG

In 1968, the New Yardbirds formed out of the ashes of, unsurprisingly, the Yardbirds. With new singer Robert Plant, drummer John Bonham, guitarist Jimmy Page and on bass John Paul 'George and Ringo' Jones, the New Yardbirds were in need of a better name. For two weeks they were the New New Yardbirds, until Keith Moon (who was hog-whimperingly pissed and saying whatever words came into his head) dubbed them 'Led Zeppelin'. Now they had a sound, a name, a look – all they needed were some songs.

Fortunately Page's enormous blues collection was an

instant inspiration, much as the contents of an unlocked safe are an inspiration to a burglar. Soon Zeppelin were regaling the world with new versions of old songs, from Willie Dixon's 'Bring It On Home' to folkie Jake Holmes's 'Dazed and Confused' (which Zep renamed 'Dazed and Confused' to avoid people thinking they'd just stolen the whole thing). But manager Peter Grant insisted the band go into the studio and record a set of original songs. 'If we manage that,' quipped Plant, 'you can call Ross McWhirter at the Guinness Book of Records.' Hence the unofficial nickname for this set.

The album begins promisingly, with an all-out assault on Willie Dixon's 'You Need Love', a version so power-ful and spacey that it almost seems churlish to point out that renaming the song 'Whole Lotta Love' is a bit, well, naughty. But there are arguably enough differences to sat-isfy the lawyers. Which cannot be said for track two, an epic seven-minute workout called 'Blues Theme from Z-Cars'. Page's guitar zooms and darts and screams behind Plant's harmonica, but even the twin thunder of Jones's bass and Bonham's drums cannot disguise the fact that 'Blues Theme from Z-Cars' is nothing more than the, er, theme from Z-Cars done really loudly and really slowly.

The band then display their love of the British folk music scene as Page straps on an acoustic, tunes it to DADGAD and provides the perfect backdrop to an extraordinary vocal performance from Plant. For many fans of Bert Jansch, Martin Carthy and even the young Bob Dylan, there is little to beat Led Zeppelin's awesome, moving, gut-wrenching classic, 'Babe We're All Going to the Zoo Tomorrow'. *Gonna see the snake*, croons Plant, *Oooh crawling kingsnake/King of the reptile house is/Living in my leather trousers*. It's a terrifying performance which would give Robert Johnson a run for his money, and would never exist if Plant hadn't been round Bonham's house that afternoon watching *Animal Magic with Johnny Morris*.

After an early attempt at 'Black Dog', whose lyrics here aren't so much similar to those of the Beatles' 'Ticket to Ride' as separated from them at birth, and a brilliant 'Immigrant Song' (marred only by a trumpet solo from Jones which if it adhered closer to the *Magic Roundabout* theme would have got pregnant by it), *McWhirter's Originals* plays its trump card; the earliest known recording of 'Stairway to Heaven'. At least, that's what the fans claim. To untrained ears it sounds like the melody from Max Bygraves's 'You Need Hands' with huge lyrical quotes ripped out of 'Oom-Pah-Pah' from the musical *Oliver!* It's undeniably effective, though, as Page scythes and riffs away and Plant sings, *Oom-pah-pah! Oom-pah-pah!* over and over again. And then, as that familiar guitar line rings out, Bonham's drums crash in and the whole thing swerves madly into the theme from *Animal Magic*. The rest of the album consists of fuzzy jams on old Shadows tunes and a most tantalising snatch of what's either 'Mannish Boy' by Muddy Waters or a major reversioning of the *Captain Pugwash* theme.

When a source close to the band helpfully pointed out

that 'dead blues men can't sue', the album was quickly shelved on a really high shelf and they made a new one. Thankfully, tapes still circulate. But not as fast as some of those dead blues men.*

---

* Circulate, as in go round or *spin*. As in spinning in a grave. Do we have to spell out every cheap joke?

1. Whole Lotta Love

2. Blues Theme from *Z-Cars*

3. Babe, We're All Going to The Zoo Tomorrow

4. Black Dog

5. Stairway to Heaven

6. Jam #1

7. Jam #2

8. Anutha Jam

9. More Jam Than Hartley's

10. Oh Good, Another Jam

11. Jam Jam Jammety Jam Jam

12. Mannish Boy (*Captain Pugwash*)

BELTER

BY

ARETHA FRANKLIN

RECORDED: 1970
PRODUCER: JERRY WEXLER
LABEL: ATLANTIC

It's a well-established fact that Aretha Franklin possesses one of the most unique and wonderful voices in the history of popular music. When she uses that sweet, mellow tone, she can make grown men cry and reassess their lives and their relationships. More importantly, she can unleash the full force of it to devastating effect. People still talk of the legendary incident when, singing gospel in her father's church at a young age, she got carried away and made a statue of Jesus pull his hands off the cross and cover his ears. Not in a bad way, though. There was also the time when she was recording at Muscle Shoals in Alabama and some members of the Klan came to pay her a visit. She gave them the full force of her High C and left them dazed, disorientated and with their pointy hats permanently wilted. With this talent it was therefore no surprise that she should come to the attention of the CIA.

In 1970 the Vietnam war was at its height. President Nixon had not yet discovered the delights of home taping, but he was becoming very unpopular. So he did what all unpopular domestic leaders do. Have a war abroad. Since Vietnam was already ongoing, he turned his attention to Cambodia. And that's when the demonstrations began at universities all across the country, most notably at Kent State. Nixon had to stop them getting out of hand. He called in his top advisers and a bold plan was hatched.

Jerry Wexler, Aretha's producer, was brought in by J. Edgar Hoover (wearing a lovely twinset, Prince Albert and pearls) and told the plan. In a nutshell, they wanted to weaponise Aretha Franklin. Wexler refused to have anything to do with it, until Hoover told him he had a recording of Wexler reading out a manual on marijuana production at a New York beat poetry night in the Fifties. Wexler was appalled – not because he had been discovered, but because it was such awful poetry. He reluctantly agreed. The Queen of Soul would record an album that would be played to students at such an intense pitch that they would immediately surrender.

Aretha was rushed into the studio to start work on the album *Belter*, and Wexler gave his instructions. Just go with the High C: big and loud and hold it as long as you can. Maybe an hour or so.

Lyrics were changed to reflect the album's true purpose.

'I Say a Little Prayer', now told from the point of view of a National Guardsman, was a prime example: *I get myself tooled up/Get ammo and load my guns up/And say a little prayer for you/But just a little one, hippy*. Another of her greatest hits received similar treatment: *S.T.U.D.E.N.T./ Get back to class immediately/Or we'll fire tear gas.* Aretha had serious qualms, but kept on singing.

'People Get Ready' changed from being a song about waiting for non-violent, positive change to one about people preparing to have their faces blown off. The peace movement was dismissed in no uncertain terms in 'Chain of Fools' and 'A Change Isn't Gonna Come' spelled out exactly what would happen to any kind of dissent against the Nixon administration. When Secretary of State Henry Kissinger was brought in to duet on 'Dr Feelgood' and turned the lyrics* into an excuse for the bombing of the Ho Chi Minh trail, Aretha, a lifelong Democrat, finally began to get angry and demand answers.

Wexler came clean and admitted everything. The studio walls shook with Aretha's angry response and her scream of rage blew the sound engineer's hat off. Taking her revenge, she penned 'I Never Hated a Man the Way I Hate You, Mr Nixon' and sang it with such controlled vitriol that Nixon's ears began bleeding, even though he was hundreds of miles away being pleasured by a White House intern. The set finished with 'Ain't No Way (I'm

---

* Kissinger, who had a notoriously atrocious singing voice, spoke the lyrics and inadvertently invented rap fifteen years early.

Gonna Let Nixon Get Away with This)'. Songs completed, Aretha stormed out of the studio and took the tapes with her, telling Wexler that if he ever told anyone about this she would play the tapes down his phone at full volume until his brains flew out of his ears.

Wexler went back to Hoover (in a fetching cream trouser suit, matching hat and purple blouse) and told him what happened. Hoover in turn told Nixon, who just shrugged.

'Oh well,' Nixon is reported to have said. 'Worth a try. Guess we'll just have to send in the National Guard and shoot the fuckers.'

1. I Say a Little Prayer
   (To Lull You into a False Sense of Security)

2. People Get Ready (To Get Your Faces Blown Off)

3. Dr Feelgood (Peace Is a Seriously Warlike Business)
   (feat. Henry Kissinger)

4. Night Time Is the Right Time (For Stealth Attacks)

5. Chain of Fools (Can't Change the World)

6. Come Back Baby (I Ain't Finished with You Yet)

7. A Change Isn't Gonna Come
   (If I Have Anything to Say about It)

8. S.T.U.D.E.N.T.

9. I Never Hated a Man the Way I Hate You, Mr Nixon

10. Ain't No Way
    (I'm Gonna Let Nixon Get Away with This)

The Uncle of Funcle.
Not on drugs

The Queen is behind you!
Oh no, she isn't!

Good evening Wembley! (IKEA)

Mumford and Sons' road crew

FLUTE WARS,
FLUFFERS
AND
FOLDING POPES

ALWAYS A DULL MOMENT

BY

ROD STEWART

RECORDED: 1976
PRODUCER: NOT PRODUCED
LABEL: RIVA/PEBBLE MILL RECORDINGS

In 1976, Rod Stewart found himself in an unusual position. Then, after Britt Ekland had gone home, he sat down to consider his situation. For years, he'd been Rod the Lad, the lovable, football-playing feathercut rock and roller, maintaining a career as solo singer and member of The Faces in a spectacular feat of keepie-uppie. But now The Faces were over, and Rod was an international rock star. His hair was blonder than a llama's arse and his roots were no longer showing. Sure, he was selling out breasts and signing stadiums (or was it the other way round? The champagne made it hard to tell) but surely there was something more to life than this?

Rod sat down on his diamond-encrusted onyx toilet and looked in the mirror. An hour later, freed from the fixating magic of his own reflection, he realised something had to be done. Summoning the cream of the world's session men to his mansion in Essex, Rod laid it on the line. After they'd all admired it, Rod put it away again and told them of his masterplan. He would record an album which laid his life bare, which revealed every moment of his waking existence. It would make Lennon's Primal Scream therapy album look like *Wings Over America*. It would be the confessional to end all confessionals.

Unfortunately, Rod hadn't realised that his life, while well-paid and extremely pleasant, lacked thrills. It was, in the parlance of the punks who'd soon come along and mock Rod and his generation, 'booooring'. Rod's lyrical skills were matched only by his melodic skills, as song after song droned on like a beautifully sung shopping list.

It begins promisingly, with a glorious yelp of *Weeeeellll!!!!* and the time-honoured bluesman's cry of *I woke up this morning ...* But that's followed by quite a long pause as Rod struggles to remember what happened next. *About half past ten*, he finally croons, *I phoned down for some toast/And coffee and that*. There then follows a saxophone solo whose enthusiasm seems wasted on the material. It gets worse. In verse two, Rod goes to the toilet, reads the paper, has a go at the crossword and gets angry with the cartoons. *I just don't get The Perishers*, he exclaims several times in what is, admittedly, the album's most emotional moment. Then Rod washes his hands and gets up.

Track two, 'What Shall I Wear Today?' is as long as it is dull. You'd think the former Rod the Mod would be able to spin a fascinating song out of the subject of schmutter, but no. Beginning with a fretful list of Y-front options, Rod launches into a list of his favourite socks: *The grey ones/The red ones/The blue ones/The other blue ones ...* that soon becomes a monotonous mantra. By the time Rod is considering which vest to wear, the listener is contemplating pulling their own ears off.

Tracks three to six deal with the thorny topic of what to do until lunchtime and are best avoided, as are tracks eight to ten, which concern what to do after lunch. Which leaves track seven, the album's highlight (if that word won't sue for misrepresentation), *'Pebble Mill at One* at One', a song about – no surprises here – sitting down at one o'clock to watch the lunchtime news and entertainment show *Pebble Mill at One*. Lines such as *I love Donny Macloud* and *Oh good, the special guest is Jilly Cooper* decorate a surprisingly funky Brazilian rhythm.

Rod saves the worst for last, the ten-minute epic 'Having My Tea', which is, oddly, a list of beers and spirits. As he slurs the final line, *Grape and grain/Oh what a pain*, we hear what appears to be his head hitting a mike-stand and the tape clicks to a halt, ensuring we don't hear the band looking for the combination to Rod's wallet so they can all get cabs home.

The next day, Rod woke up, sobered up and wised up.

He'd never attempt a personal record again. As he stood in his luxury home, listening to David 'Diddy' Hamilton on his solid gold radio, he must have reflected, 'You know what? There isn't more to life than this.'

1. Time to Get Up (Nooo, Don't Wanna)

2. What Shall I Wear Today?

3. Ooh Biccies!

4. Let's Pretend the Swirls on the Carpet Are Snakes

5. What's the Recipe Today, Jim?

6. Is That the Postman? Yes It Is, It's the Postman! Oh ... It's Not the Postman

7. *Pebble Mill at One* at One

8. Old Black and White Film on BBC2

9. A Walk around the Garden

10. Dog Poo on My New Shoe

11. Having My Tea

LAS VEGAS SKYLINE

BY

BOB DYLAN & LIBERACE

RECORDED: 1969
PRODUCER: BOB JOHNSTON
LABEL: COLUMBIA

In 1969, Bob Dylan was tired. The pressures of fame and of being the poster boy for everything from civil rights to the anti-war movement to guide dogs was getting him down. His flirtations with rock, with country and with motorbikes had alienated him from the Newport folkies, and now he wanted to finally sever his connections with those fans who still wanted him to wear a silly cap and blow harmonica. The times were indeed a-changing; but nobody could anticipate Dylan's next move. He'd worked with The Band, he'd worked with Johnny Cash, but he still couldn't shake off the crazy stalkers who saw him as the Folk Messiah.

And then Dylan went to Caesar's Palace, Las Vegas, to see Elvis Presley . . .

Nobody knows if Bob wanted to see Elvis as a fan, for a joke, or with a more serious plan in mind; nobody knows because Dylan never saw Presley. That night, Elvis was back in Memphis, recording his Comeback Special. So Dylan, who had time to kill and nothing else to do, went next door to the Silver Dollar, and saw Liberace.

At this point in his career, Liberace was the ivory-tinkling, pearly-grinned Queen of Kitsch. His sugary reworkings of popular classics were loved by the old and the uncool everywhere. He was show business incarnate. He was, in short, the polar opposite of Bob Dylan.

That night, somebody asked Bob if he'd like to go backstage and 'say hi to Lee'. The scene is recounted, with some artistic licence, in the movie *Behind the Candelabra*, where Michael Douglas's Liberace is surprised and suspicious to find Johnny Depp's Dylan lurking in the corner of his dressing room. The movie paints the moment as a clash of opposites united, bizarrely, by Bob's fondness for Liberace's version of Mrs Zimmerman's favourite song, 'Buttons and Bows'. We can only imagine what really happened.

We do know that, a week later, a silver-plated Rolls-Royce pulled up outside Gold Star Studios in Los Angeles and its occupant floated inside in a cloud of furs and cologne. The Gold Star engineers had never seen anything like it, and when Dylan turned up an hour later in a buck-skin coat with a battered acoustic guitar, they steeled themselves for a terrible session. But they were wrong. From the opening bars of 'Like a Rolling Rhinestone', where Liberace and a school choir add a sugar rush to Dylan's original; to the final, almost angelic release of 'Amazing Grace', where Dylan's heartfelt whine and simple acoustic rise up to meet Liberace's churchy keys, *Las Vegas Skyline* is a remarkable record. Those of us lucky enough to have heard it, either on its original Yellow Dog vinyl bootleg or on the few numbers doled out in miserly fashion on *Dylan's Chronicles* Vol. 6, will never forget it.

Liberace never mentioned the recording, although for a few years afterwards he did sport a Dylanesque cap in private (albeit a rhinestone-studded leather one) and sometimes included the album's music-box reworking of 'The Times They Are A-Changing' in his set. As for Dylan, only the presence of a shades-wearing, pencil-moustached figure among the mourners at Liberace's funeral testified to one of the strangest moments in an already very strange career.

1. Like a Rolling Rhinestone

2. Tangled Up in a Blue Velveteen Jumpsuit

3. Codpiece of Spanish Leather

4. Forever Young
   (Thanks to Martin Blomberg MD, ASPS)

5. My Face It Is A-Changing

6. Leopard Skin Pill-Box Hat with Feathers On and a
   Little Waterfall on Top

7. Hey Mr Grand Piano Man

8. The Mighty Queen
   (Featuring Liberace's 'Waltzing' Waters)

9. The Lovely Dress of Hattie Carroll

10. Absolutely Sweet Little Old Lady Marie

11. Ballad of a Thin Man (Wearing a Sparkly Girdle)

12. Just Like a Woman (How *Dare* You!)

13. Amazing Grace (Trad.)

SUCKING OFF
TRAMPS IN THE PARK

BY
THE POGUES

RECORDED: 1987
PRODUCER: SHANE MACGOWAN
LABEL: ISLAND

In light of the rumoured Pogues musical being written by the creative forces behind HBO's *The Wire*, it may be enlightening – and perhaps cautionary – to revisit an earlier attempt by the band's guiding light and frontman.

In 1986, someone spiked Shane MacGowan's drink. To this day no one knows who or with what, but given that he'd been on a week-long mission to rid the Borough of Camden of alcohol by drinking it all, it must have been something rather impressive. And someone very brave. But whatever it was, it propelled MacGowan to even greater heights of artistic creation. 'I just sat on the bridge at

Camden Lock, danglin' me feet over the side,' MacGowan later recalled. 'An' I had this epiphany. Nearly fell in the water.' Then he made that laugh that sounds like Mutley crossed with a psychotic Catherine wheel coming loose from its moorings.

He saw the next project for the Pogues unfold before him. A concept album, distilling the whole of the Irish immigrant experience in London, filtered through his own unique songwriting sensibilities and his own idiosyncratic world-view. As Irish as anything could be, created by someone born in Tunbridge Wells.

The action would take place over one night. Fintan, a young Irish poet, comes to London to seek his fortune. But things don't go as planned. He falls on hard times, gets involved with booze, drugs and unsavoury characters. And, in a heartbreaking climax, ends up performing the titular activity.

MacGowan got straight to work, rousing the rest of the band from their beds, even though it was half past three in the morning, and ushering them straight into the studio to begin work on the songs he had already written. He also called in several Irish, or Eire-satz, performers to guest on the album. For the track 'Dirty Old Man' Elvis Costello sang the role of Uncle Brian, an ageing, bespectacled tramp who tries to steal young women away with his pseudo-philosophical wordsmithery. 'Body of an Armenian', an imagined revenge fantasy, drew on an altercation Fintan once had with a landlord who cruelly evicted him from his flat for setting it on fire.

Halfway through recording it, MacGowan realised an album wasn't big enough to contain the scope of his ambitions and decided it should be a musical instead. The album would work as a calling card to attract investors. The first song he recorded in these new sessions was 'If I Should Fail to Start a Fight', a subtle, nuanced examination of the Irish character as he saw it. Sinead O'Connor contributed a track in character as a down-at-heel whore who still retained an abiding love for the Catholic church and a heart of gold: 'I'm a Pope You Don't Meet Every Day'.

The masterstroke, as MacGowan then saw it, would be having a narrator. He first approached Seamus Heaney who declined, then Dave Allen, who did likewise. In desperation, he turned to rotund Northern Irish comedian Frank Carson. The relationship soon soured as Carson started to put his own ad libs to MacGowan's poetry: *I've said goodbye to open fields/And skies that sing with summer blue/Exchanged them for the dull embrace/Of London's grit and smoky hue/Its people stern and closed of face/Friendship veneer and lacquer/But I've got this bird with massive tits/I tell you, she's a cracker!*

The climactic title song would be Shane's triumph as a songwriter. The production would be lush, with a choir and full orchestra. It would be the most haunting, beautiful melody every written. He called in Kirsty McColl to duet with him and the rest should have been history. *The middle of the night babe/On Hampstead Heath/You took out your cock, dear/I took out me teeth* was just one such couplet the pair attacked with relish. But by this time the rest of the band had had enough. Spider Stacey took MacGowan to one side and repeatedly hit him over the head with a tin tray until he saw sense and the project was abandoned.

Most of the songs were salvaged for the next studio album, *If I Should Fall from Grace with God*, and Kirsty McColl brought in her then husband, Steve Lillywhite to get the sessions back on track. However MacGowan couldn't stop thinking about *Sucking Off Tramps in the Park*. He loved the tune so much that he hastily rewrote the lyrics and, using both McColl and the same backing track, re-recorded it as 'Fairytale of New York'.

The rest is history.

1. Body of an Armenian

2. Dirty Old Man (feat. Elvis Costello)

3. If I Should Fail to Start a Fight

4. Waxy's Dangle

5. I'm a Pope You Don't Meet Every Day
   (feat. Sinead O'Connor)

6. A Pair of Crossed Eyes

7. The Old Man in Drag

8. The Wild Hats of Camden Town

9. Streets of Sorrow/Birmingham's Shit

10. Sucking Off Tramps in the Park (feat. Kirsty McColl)

AN AFTERNOON AT THE OPTICIANS

BY

QUEEN

RECORDED: 1986
PRODUCER: ROY THOMAS BAKER
LABEL: EMI

In the early months of 1986, Freddie Mercury was troubled. Having demonstrated their chops as a live band with a show-stealing performance at Live Aid, Queen had been searching for a new direction as recording artists. Inspiration came at last courtesy of a bizarre and much talked about accident. While reaching for a Jaffa Cake at his birthday party, Mercury tripped over one of his infamous 'coke-dwarves' and was badly poked in the eye. Exactly *what* poked him in the eye has been the subject of much conjecture, though Brian May has always insisted it was a large sausage on a stick. A week wearing a diamond-studded eye-patch alerted the toothy showman to the plight of those with severe optical problems. This, combined with a desire to make a record that would resonate with 'ordinary' people, led to the making of the legendary album that would complete the trilogy begun with *A Night at the Opera* and *A Day at the Races*.

Musically, *Opticians* is less grandiose than its predecessors, though many have singled out Brian May's twelve-minute acoustic odyssey 'Cataracts on the Windows of My Soul' as one of the more pretentious songs Queen ever recorded. May, who constructed a new guitar from used spectacle frames especially for the recording, has spoken since of his desire to use 'glaucoma as, you know ... a kind of metaphor' in order to comment more widely on alienation, gender warfare and walking into things. A bold ambition certainly, but one that is only partially successful, thanks to lyrics such as, *Tiresias saw more clearly/Than those who could actually see/Now, we need the blind prophet more than ever/Though these days he would probably have a dog ...*

The recording sessions were difficult to say the least, thanks to Mercury's insistence that, in order to *really* feel what it was like to be blind, the band had to wear bags over their heads. There was chaos in the control room, a good deal of inadvertent touching and several awkward moments that unfortunately found their way on to the finished master tapes. The middle-eight of 'Blurred Vision' is somewhat compromised when John Deacon tells Freddie to 'watch where he's bloody going' and, as 'I'm

Going Slightly Blind' is fading out, Mercury's sensitive piano ceding ground beautifully to an eerie mandolin lick, it comes to an abrupt halt as Brian May falls into Roger Taylor's drum kit. With myopic inevitability, David Bowie (at his most chameleon-like) does exactly the same thing halfway through the album's stunning closer.

An Afternoon at the Opticians received a mixed reception when it was premiered live at Belgium's *Tool-Rock* festival in late 1986. Mercury insisted that the songs were performed in total darkness, but when the band stumbled back on for an encore of 'We Are the Champions', the lights came up to reveal that all but a handful of the aggrieved Belgians had gone home.

With both Baker and his engineer also forced to work in the dark it could be no surprise to anyone that the finished album sounded so atrocious. However, more than a quarter of a century after it was shelved, it certainly merits another listen. As an homage to Mercury's original concept, many prefer to do so with a blindfold on.

And their hands over their ears.

1. A G F D H K C M T P L Q

2. Fat-Bottomed Ophthalmologist

3. I See a Little Silhouetto
   (I Need A Stronger Prescription)

4. Blurred Vision

5. Cataracts on the Window of My Soul

6. I See a Massive Silhouetto (Still Not Right)

7. I'm in Love with My Optrex

8. Where's the Silhouetto Gone? (Looks Like Bifocals)

9. I'm Going Slightly Blind

10. Under Pressure Thanks to Ocular Hypertension

POPE
ORIGAMI

BY

SINEAD O'CONNOR

RECORDED: 1993
PRODUCER: SINEAD O'CONNOR/RYUCHI SAKATATA
LABEL: CHRYSALIS VIDEO

One of the earliest video albums, this long-suppressed collection sees O'Connor at her most controversial. It followed hot on the heels of her notorious appearance on *Saturday Night Live* during which she forgot the lyrics to 'Nothing Compares 2 U' and improvised by tearing up a picture of Pope John Paul II she found in her pocket. O'Connor quickly saw that there was mileage in the idea. 'I just woke up one day and thought, there's *loads* of Popes,' she told *Rolling Stone* in 1995, 'and lots of things to do with the pieces after I'd torn the photos up.' Once she had secured the services of the ageing, much-revered

Sakatata – a former Shinto monk and the acknowledged master of contemporary paper-folding – she set about recording the series of short videos that became the legendary and profoundly shocking *Pope Origami*.

The idea was a simple one. O'Connor would tear up photographs of assorted pontiffs and then Sakatata would fashion the pieces into objects symbolic of topics close to O'Connor's heart – spirituality, the systematic abuse of power, and shagging. 'I wanted to show that destruction was not always a bad thing, that it could lead to beauty and to the creation of something powerful,' she said later. 'Also, I just really fucking enjoyed tearing them up, you know?'

Never one for doing things by halves, O'Connor prepared for the shoot by immersing herself thoroughly in Japanese culture. She lived on rice, took up Sumo and bought schoolgirls' pants on the internet, so that she could burn them. As a comment on the subjugation of geishas, she spent the months before recording with her feet tightly bound, but this meant that she kept falling over during filming and had to be propped up at all times.

On those few, fuzzy VHS copies of *Pope Origami* that survive, O'Connor certainly cuts a powerful figure. Dressed in a willow-pattern boiler suit bedecked with bandoliers, she stares defiantly into camera as each photograph is displayed for a few seconds before being torn into pieces. As if this were not shocking enough, O'Connor chants a few well-chosen words in an eerie and deeply affecting monotone as each picture is ripped: *Evil .../Evil .../Evil .../A right nasty bugger, he is/Bloody hell, look at this one* etc.

The album builds powerfully, until the fifth video, which even the most generous of critics have agreed is tragically flawed. We see immediately that O'Connor's research has not been as rigorous as it might have been when she rips up a photo of a Ku Klux Klan member, mistaking his pointed hood for a popish mitre. This misunderstanding seems trivial however when we reach the final video, in which O'Connor triumphantly holds aloft a picture of blue-eyed soul boy Darryl Hall, which appears to have been chosen simply because he has big hair.

As far as the relationship between O'Connor and Mr Sakatata goes, the cracks are there for all to see – or rather to *hear*, as all we see of the gentle origami master are his beautifully manicured hands, as he skilfully folds, nips and pinches the photographic fragments into detailed, if shocking shapes.

The exchange just before the third video is typical:

Sakatata: Can I not just do a flapping bird?
O'Connor: No.
Sakatata: But I do a lovely flapping bird.
O'Connor: Shut the fuck up and fold!

It is as a direct result of legal action taken by Sakatata that *Pope Origami* was never released and is now a highly collectable item. Sakatata made his feelings abundantly clear in his 2007 autobiography *My Unfolding Life*:

> I am an artist ... a poet of paper. Through paper I express what is in my heart and in my soul. I was *not* happy making paper genitals ...

1. Pope Innocent I Becomes a Dove of Peace

2. Pope Boniface III Becomes Something That Could Be a Star, It's Hard to Tell

3. Pope Benedict IX Becomes a Cock and Balls

4. Pope Leo X Becomes the Soul of a Tortured Child (Might Be a Dog)

5. Unnamed Man in a Pointy Hat Becomes a Cloud

6. Pope Adrian II with His Face Folded Over So He Looks Like Tommy Cooper

7. Pope Pius IV Becomes a Vagina

8. Pope Gregory XVI Becomes a Clenched Fist

9. Darryl Hall Becomes a Lovely Heart

ALAN THOMPSON

BY

ELVIS COSTELLO

RECORDED: 1977
PRODUCER: NICK LOWE
LABEL: STIFF

In 1977, the *NME*'s Nick Kent interviewed up-and-coming new wave icon Elvis Costello. Frothing with amphetamine sulphate and cider, Costello spat at Kent that he was motivated by 'revenge and guilt', a made-to-measure slogan that Kent duly reported. But what nobody could have known was that Elvis was motivated by a third emotion: a burning hatred of one man in particular; a man whose very existence provided inspiration, perspiration and respiration to Mister Hate Specs for over thirty years.

We don't know when Costello's obsession with the man history knows as 'Alan Thompson' began, but it must have been around the time Costello formed his first band, Flip City. Demos – collected here on this bootleg album – showcase his hatred in primitive form. There's no sign of the sophisticated wordsmith of *Imperial Bedroom* here as, using the tune of what would later become 'Radio Sweetheart', Costello sings, *Sing one time for that bastard Alan Thompson/Punch him in the clock and run away quick*. Then there's 'The Angels Hate Alan Thompson Too', soon to be rewritten as 'Red Shoes' – *Well, he used to be disgusting/And he still is, through and through/Oh yeah, the angels hate Alan Thompson too*.

Most searing of all, and a song that many Costellophiles consider to be the central clue to the mystery, is 'Alan's Sin (My Aim Is True)'. *I'm not trying to go totally mental*, sings Elvis in a psychopath's croon, *But I'd shove you onto the Northern Line*. What is Alan's 'sin'? Is it something to do with wedding cake? Nobody knows. Even a chance remark in Bruce Thomas's unauthorised on-the-road Costello memoir *The Big Wheel* – 'Some big-nosed bloke in glasses called Alan came backstage tonight. Elvis went white and hid in the bog' – merely adds to the bafflement.

Whatever it is, Costello clearly could not let it lie. Song after song repeats the theme. 'I Don't Want to Go to Alan Thompson's House', 'Accidents Will Happen to Alan Thompson', 'Alan Thompson Shot with His Own Gun', 'You Little Fool Alan Thompson', 'Everyday I Write to Alan Thompson (And Tell Him to Fuck Off)', 'Indoor Fireworks inside Alan Thompson's Mouth' – the list is endless. But the pattern is clear. Costello, stuck for a new direction or song-writing idea, just thinks of Alan

Thompson and *hey presto*, he has a song. Tweaking the lyrics for the radio, he then has a hit.

It was a unique working method and it worked – right up to the famed McCartney/MacManus Sessions, where Costello became the new writing partner of Paul 'Macca' McCartney. Things went well at first, until Paul started to notice a pattern. He'd supply a melody and it would come back with some very unidirectional Costello lyrics. 'My Brave Face Hates Alan Thompson's Cowardly Face', 'Alan Thompson Should Change His Name to Veronica Because He's a Girl', 'I Want Her to Hit Alan Thompson' – it was too much for the genial scouser who, muttering, 'This is worse than John in 1970', told Costello he had a simple choice: get help with his Alan Thompson obsession or go back to working with The Jags.

Costello took the hint. Since then, he's settled down, married jazz artist Diane Krall and watched as a new generation of fans fall in love with his music. Some say the fire's gone out. Others wonder if he'll ever be the Angry Young Man of yore again. But some say: where's Alan Thompson when we need him?

1. Sing One Time for Alan Thompson
2. The Angels Hate Alan Thompson Too
3. Alan's Sin (My Aim Is True)
4. Watching the Detectives Look for Alan Thompson's Body
5. Blame It on Alan Thompson
6. I Don't Want to Go to Alan Thompson's House
7. Pump It up Alan Thompson's Arse
8. Accidents Will Happen (To Alan Thompson)
9. I Can't Stand Alan Thompson (For Falling Down)
10. Alan Thompson Shot with His Own Gun
11. You Little Fool Alan Thompson
12. Everyday I Write to Alan Thompson
    (And Tell Him to Fuck Off)
13. An Alan Thompson Out of Time
14. The Only Flame in Town Is Burning
    Alan Thompson's House Down
15. I Want You (To Shoot Alan Thompson)
16. Indoor Fireworks inside Alan Thompson's Mouth
17. My Brave Face Hates Alan Thompson's Cowardly Face
18. Alan Thompson Should Change His Name to
    Veronica Because He's a Girl
19. I Want Her to Shoot Alan Thompson
20. 13 Steps Lead Down to Alan Thompson's Tomb
21. Tear Off Alan Thompson's Head (It's a Doll Revolution)
22. She

DODECAHEDRON

BY

**GABRIEL, COLLINS, BANKS,
HACKETT, RUTHERFORD, FRIPP,
BRUFORD, MUIR, WETTON, CROSS,
GILMOUR, WATERS, WRIGHT,
MASON, WAKEMAN, SQUIRE, HOWE,
WHITE, ANDERSON, ANDERSON,
EVAN, HAMMOND, BARRE, BARLOW,
PUGH, PUGH, BARNEY MCGREW,
CUTHBERT, DIBBLE, GRUB,
EMERSON, LAKE AND PALMER**

RECORDED: 1974
PRODUCER: STEVE HILLAGE
LABEL: MANTICORE/CHARISMA

Late in 1974, the greatest prog-rock supergroup ever assembled gathered at Island studios in London. The line-up was simply staggering, featuring assorted members of Genesis, ELP, Pink Floyd, Yes and Jethro Tull, as well as a couple of blokes with funny haircuts nobody knew, who had wandered in off the streets wearing greatcoats, smelling of skunk and muttering about hobbits. The idea was a simple one – to make the ultimate prog concept album. The recording session that followed would become the stuff of legend and the long-lost, long (really long) player that these heroes of prog produced would make *The Lamb Lies Down on Broadway* sound like the first Ramones single.

Arguments over songwriting credits began before you could say 'mellotron' and it quickly became clear that not even a triple album would be long enough. So, amid the in-fighting and drug-taking, the concept of *Dodecahedron** was born: a ten-disc, double-grooved, twenty-sided album featuring one sprawling track in twenty 'movements', that would give each musician time and space to express their individual visions, to demonstrate their instrumental virtuosity and to sing about pixies a bit.

'Yes, there were tensions,' producer Steve Hillage told *Gandalf* magazine in the early eighties. 'With everyone sharing songwriting credits, they all wanted to have their own way. I remember Roger Waters getting really pissed off when Robert Fripp took three and a half hours to play one chord. It looked like it was going to get nasty.' Exactly *how* nasty it became remains unclear, as Hillage

---

*A dodecahedron is of course a twelve-sided object. This was pointed out by the bass player from Caravan who went on to let everyone know that a twenty-sided object is, in fact, called an icosahedron. Everyone else was far too stoned to pay any attention.

admits that he had fallen asleep before things came to a head. Though he does remember that when he finally woke up, Fripp was wincing and had what looked like a nasty Chinese burn.

The most memorable altercation, however, was documented in detail by Yes keyboard wizard Wakeman in his loveably grumpy memoir *Prog Rick*. The incident involved the flamboyant frontmen of Genesis and Jethro Tull and began, according to the book, with a minor argument as to who would play a particular flute solo:

> Gabriel clearly fancied having a bash, but Ian Anderson was having none of it. They had sort of a 'flute off' . . . a 'duelling flutes' kind of thing, but when that didn't settle it things became a bit more personal. Anderson told Gabriel that his hair looked really stupid with that bit shaved off at the front. It did, but the rest of us had been too polite to say anything. Gabriel made some snide comment about a codpiece and . . . you know, it just kicked off. Gabriel put his fists up, all Queensberry rules, public school stuff. But Anderson's Scottish, so he just nutted him . . .
>
> *Prog Rick*, Random House, 1993

If the album was unique, then its packaging was suitably extravagant. There clearly needed to be a *lot* of it, just to fit all the names on, but nobody could have foreseen quite how excessive things would become. Hipgnosis designed a complex series of sleeves within sleeves within sleeves that would, when opened and folded in the mathematically correct sequence, form themselves into a twenty-sided object or dodecahedron. The artwork contained one hundred and eighty-seven separate riddles, pictograms and number puzzles which, when solved, revealed a further thirty-three-and-a-third hidden messages in cuneiform, hieroglyphs and masonic symbols. Successful deciphering of these allowed the album's owner to release one side, flap or corner of the dodecahedron. It was, by any stretch of the imagination, a tad overwrought, and is one of the many reasons why this prog-rock masterwork remains almost entirely unheard to this day.

Proggers queued for hours to purchase the album(s) but sadly none but a handful were ever able to listen to it. Many laboured for days without a break to open the cover, resulting in several nervous breakdowns, a great many divorces and at least one tragic death from malnutrition. By the time the first fan had successfully pieced *Dodecahedron* together and released the vinyl, many of the musicians involved had already denounced the album altogether and were running fish farms.

And punk had arrived.

1. Dodecahedron (14 hours, 21 minutes, 7 seconds)

WE HURT TOO

BY
**BRUCE SPRINGSTEEN &
THE WALL-STREET BAND**

RECORDED: 2009
PRODUCER: BRENDAN O'BRIEN
LABEL: CBS (UNRELEASED)

The financial crisis of 2008 affected many people, none more so than Bruce Springsteen who subsequently spent three months visiting some of the hardest-hit areas – Beverly Hills, Palm Beach, Malibu – before settling down at his ranch (otherwise known as Colorado) to record what would become the holy grail for Springsteen collectors – *We Hurt Too* – an album that has spurred more rumour, scuttlebutt, and delusional fantasy than perhaps any other.

Thematically, *We Hurt Too* is the third part of the trilogy begun with *Nebraska* and continued on *The Ghost of Tom Joad*. Stylistically, however, Springsteen daringly decides to eschew his trademark acoustic guitar for a full orchestra and classical soloists. (A rough mix circulates of 'Born to Run a Multinational' with Nigel Kennedy's violin clearly audible as Springsteen sings: *Just strap your hands cross my financial instruments/Together we can break this bank*.)

The album kicks off with lead single 'We Hurt Too'. Typical for Springsteen, the song is both an anthem for the defeated and a rallying cry. The shift from singing about immigrant farmhands and rent boys to investment bankers and CEOs is barely noticeable.

'The Yard' tells the story of Miles and Francesca – falling in love at Harvard Yard, finishing their MBAs and entering the world of money and triple-mortgages. Each verse skilfully unravels the golden threads of their marriage. Miles's redundancy forces them to sell the yacht, the Hamptons beach cottage and Lear jet. All they're left with is the memory of who they were and just how far they've drifted from those people (and, of course, a generous retirement package worth three million dollars a year, with annuities). This is one of the Boss's most tender and harrowing tales. Only the hardest of hearts could fail to melt at lines such as: *We learned pretty fast baby what it means to be poor/Can't buy an island in the Caribbean no more.*

'This Land is My Land', Springsteen's radical co-opting of the Woody Guthrie standard, and the epic 'The Ghost of Henry Ford' recount tales of hardship among the robber barons; 'Taxman on My Tail' sports a wonderful guest vocal from Bono; 'Johnny 99 Million' is a sly nod back to *Nebraska*, except this time the Johnny in question is an investment banker who engages in insider dealing so he can keep up the payments on his seventeen horses and $3,000-a-day cocaine habit.

Renowned musicologist Bernie Madoff has written a book-length treatise on the album and it is worth quoting from: 'Too little thought is given to the sufferings of the enormously wealthy, especially in this economic climate. We demonise them so we don't have to confront their humanity, just as we did with the poor for so many centuries.' Springsteen was one of the few ready and willing to confront that humanity and, in typically philanthropic fashion, had planned to donate a large percentage of the album's profits to a hedge fund Donald Trump had told him about. Sadly, Bruce's dream of a televised benefit concert – Banker Aid – never came to fruition, despite the enthusiastic support of both The Eagles and Billy Joel.

With *We Hurt Too* Springsteen once again shows his unique ability to empathise with the most neglected and forgotten members of society. For the first time, he writes about what it means to *actually* be The Boss and about the terrible hardships that come with the role – notably, earning more money than everyone else and firing people. Poignant and powerful, it is Springsteen finally accepting who he is – one of the richest men in the world – and coming to terms with all this entails.

1. We Hurt Too

2. Born with an ISA

3. Plunder Road

4. Lehmann Brothers under the Bridge

5. Taxman on My Tail (feat. Bono)

6. Glory Days (Are Over)

7. Johnny 99 Million

8. Born to Run a Multinational

9. Your Problems Are Not My Problems (So Shut Up)

10. Trading in the Streets

11. This Land is My Land (Trespassers Will Be Shot)

12. The Ghost of Henry Ford

13. The Last Tycoon (Elegy for Donald Trump)

VELVET UNDERGROUND & LULU

VELVET UNDERGROUND & LULU

RECORDED: 1966
PRODUCER: WARHOL
LABEL: ACETATE (UNRELEASED)

By 1965, the Velvet Underground were the most avant-garde, experimental and confrontational band on the LA scene. Lou Reed had filleted some of modern literature's finest cuts and turned them into dark hymns to drugs, degradation and dehydration. John Cale came from a background that included collaborating with La Monte Young on a 44-day-long piece consisting of a teaspoon being banged against an empty milk bottle every 122 seconds, and squeezing sheep on stage with British enfant terrible Cornelius Cardew (better known for his role in the *Planet of the Apes* films). But Reed and Cale had got bored with noise. They were tired of hypnotic drones and feedback squalls. And, besides, their ears hurt.

Late at night they discussed the music closest to their hearts – Folk and Country & Western. Anyone who picked up 1995's *Peel Slowly & See* can still remember how startled they were on hearing the disc of 1965 demos. It was recognisably Lou Reed and John Cale. It was recognisable songs – 'Venus in Furs' and 'I'm Waiting for My Man' – but they were done in a semi-acoustic, ersatz-Dylan/Country style. Listeners scratched their heads and wondered how, in the space of six months, the VU had gone from this to their icily nihilistic first album.

Enter Andy Warhol, who immediately saw that what the group needed was a female singer with a bit of spunk. 'You're fuckin' kiddin' me?' was Lou Reed's initial reply, followed by: 'Who the fuck is Lulu?', followed by Reed storming out of the studio in a sulk and scoring some lemon sherbet in Harlem. Warhol, asked about his controversial decision to bring in the Glaswegian songstress in *Kum* magazine, said: 'Repetition.' And then he said it again and again until the interviewer lost interest and left. 'It's all about repetition,' he added eight hours later. 'The name. Lu. Lu. Say it once. Say it twice. It's the same. See? Say it three times my mother used to say to me. Okay? Want a carrot?'

Sessions were fractious to say the least. Reed and Cale showed Lulu the songs they'd earmarked for their first album, songs such as 'Heroin', 'Femme Fatale' and 'Black

Angel's Death Song'. 'It's all a bit grim, pal,' Lulu shook her head as she read through them. 'What are you, fifteen years old? You need a bit of cheering up, you do,' she said, and when Reed protested she head-butted him.

A strict regime was set. The band were to be at the studio by nine sharp. After cups of tea (Cale initially refused, being a coffee man, but when Lulu upended an entire mug of scalding Darjeeling on his crotch, he wisely decided to acquire the taste). 'You're the unhealthiest bunch o' bastards I've seen in a long time,' Lulu said and forced them to eat full Glaswegian breakfasts, consisting of seven sausages, fourteen rashers of bacon, an entire black pudding, haggis, chips and something that nobody could identify – in batter.

Recording in a badly-lit basement with rats chewing their feet, Gerard Malanga spanking a pineapple, Paul Morrissey eating a cat, and a full company of fluffers, they laid down the songs that make up the legendary *Velvet Underground & Lulu* acetate. As they played their new country-folk arrangements they noticed that Lulu was changing the words. They stopped to correct her, but before Lou could get a word in, she'd glassed him.

Reed and Cale grew increasingly frustrated. Lulu was turning dark, mordant vignettes into raucous sing-alongs, with an extended, throaty, *we—eee—llll—* added for good measure at the start of every line. As their resentment grew, the music they were playing became spikier, more dissonant, angry, raw and loud enough to drown out the strangled effusions emanating from Lulu's throat. But somehow gold was struck and with a sleeve designed by Warhol featuring a deep-fried Mars bar (you could unzip the batter), the album is a delight from start to finish. 'I'm Waiting for My Nan' is a touching take on how long it takes pensioners to use the loo: *I'm waiting for my nan/Twenty-six shopping coupons in my hand*. Lulu's dulcet tones shimmer on the lovely 'Femme Fantastique'. A summer yachting trip around the Mediterranean is celebrated on 'European Fun' and Lulu's devotion to macrobiotics gives us 'Black Angel Health Song'.

Warhol listened to the tapes and found them too raw for his taste and not manufactured enough. He made the ground-breaking film *Pick* (1965) featuring a close-up of Lulu picking her nose for fifteen hours, then summarily fired the band. It is worth nothing, however, that despite their differences Lou Reed elected to name his final album *LULU*.

1. I'm Waiting for My Nan

2. Femme Fantastique

3. Heroin (No, Thanks)

4. The Christmas Gift

5. Why I Like White Sweets

6. Remus in Furs

7. European Fun

8. Black Angel Health Song

9. Lulu Lou

REVISIT THE PIG

BY

RADIOHEAD

RECORDED: 2008
PRODUCER: THOM YORKE
LABEL: BOOTLEG

When Radiohead left Parlophone, their home of some fifteen years, to carve out a career in dubtronica and gabbastep, they were enraged to learn that their erstwhile label were releasing a *Best of Radiohead* compilation album. They were even more enraged when they discovered that this so-called 'compilation' would be comprised entirely of hit singles and catchy album tracks enjoyed by the band's many fans. Singer and self-styled 'crash test dummy loser king' Thom Yorke was, perhaps unsurprisingly, the most annoyed at this appalling act of treachery, akin to the bombing of Pearl Harbor or the time he lost his Cure album and his mum wouldn't help him look for it (this latter action forming the basis of solo single 'Mum Robot Cowdroid').

There was clearly only one sane reaction to Parlophone's evil decision. Kill The Man! But after meetings with their lawyers – in which it was explained to Radiohead that a) killing The Man is a crime known as murder and b) The Man doesn't actually exist, which caused Radiohead to in turn argue that if The Man doesn't exist, it can't be a crime to kill him, at which point their lawyer, an actual man, killed himself – Johnny Greenwood had an idea. After a few minutes spent remodelling the idea so that Thom would think it was his, Greenwood had won the band over: they would show Parlophone So-Called Records what was what by rerecording their own songs and releasing their own *Best of Radiohead*!

'That'll show The Man!' crowed Yorke and, throwing some Fair Trade dollars at the corpse of their lawyer, the band went into the studio to do what they do best: spend two years on a drum sound. Eventually they became so bored that they were forced to compile a list of songs which would most benefit from a reversioning – or, as Yorke put it, 'a new bat bat batter pig pig meat dead meat new'.

The project took seven years – which is about six months in Radiohead years – during which time the band had families, fell in and out of love with Angry Birds, and even had a bizarre meeting with Cliff Richard, who, according to Greenwood, dropped by the studio one day to see 'how it was done'. It went badly. Yorke accused Richard of being 'Jeezy Cheesy', while Cliff was unimpressed with the combative Thom. 'The singer,' said Richard of Yorke, 'fought battles in vain.'

Eventually, in a massive burst of energy, the album was completed as though a volcano of creativity had exploded over the studio and showered everyone involved in rock lava. An astonishing five tracks were recorded, or rather rerecorded, or rather 'new bat bat batter pig pig meat dead meat new'-ed.

From the opener – a mix-out of 'Creep' composed entirely of radio static through which Thom Yorke's treated voice can be heard asking for a biscuit – to the closer, a mariachi-step glambient house re-imagining of 'Paranoid Android' (complete with a searing guitar solo from Professor Brian Cox), *Revisit The Pig* looks at Radiohead's career through a glass, darkly. Very darkly. Which is why it was rejected by Radiohead's record company, something the band never really came to terms with, even after their new lawyer pointed out that they *were* their own record company, before killing himself.

1. Creep (Hiss This Mix)

2. Fake Plastic Trees (Sir Humpalot Mix)

3. Anyone Can Play Guitar (Billy Tits-Out Dub)

4. How to Disappear Completely
   (Reggae Reggae Sauce Mix)

5. Paranoid Android (Tijuana Dance With Me?
   Top-Down Megamash. feat. Ke$ha)

Not a Pope

Freddie Mercury after getting poked
in the eye with a 'sausage'

Rod (without the faeces)

The only known photo of Elvis Costello (with guitar)
and Alan Thompson

KYLIE, KANT
AND A
KRAFTWERK
KRISTMAS

TRANS-POLAR EXPRESS

BY

KRAFTWERK

RECORDED: 1976
PRODUCER: HERMAN SCHTUDENDORFF
LABEL: KLING KLANG/DING DONG

'We had always wanted to record a Christmas album,' says former Kraftwerk member Karl Bartos. 'Christmas is a big event in Germany and we were fascinated by the whole process. The big questions, such as, how does Santa deliver so many toys? How can the Elves manufacture so many toys so quickly, and how does Santa determine his naughty and his nice lists? And then we realised: Santa is efficient, just like Kraftwerk. Santa uses technology, just like Kraftwerk. And Santa, like Kraftwerk, is *modern*.'

Recorded in the summer of 1976, *Trans-Polar Express* is Kraftwerk at their most festive, i.e. not very festive at all.

They *did* dress up as Santa Clauses, but this almost led to their arrest (in West Germany, prematurely getting yourself up as Father Christmas is illegal under the notorious *Zufruhsantalegen* or Premature Santa Claus Clause). They also bought some electronically triggered crackers and bedecked their sweltering Kling-Klang studio with flickering Xmas lights and a wipe-clean Xmas tree.

In just four ground-breaking tracks this legendary album sees the spirit of Christmas reduced to a series of repetitive synth patterns, some drumpad-triggered sleigh bells, and a very real sense that, above all else, this is the season for the mechanised production of consumer goods.

The album begins brilliantly with 'We Are the Elves', in which Kraftwerk, singing in vocodered high-pitched voices like a quartet of android Smurfs, declaim their festive manifesto: *We are the elves/We are the elves/We make toys to put on shelves/We will work until we drop/Death is all that makes us stop*. A catchy synth riff makes this the album's toe-tapping single. It's followed by 'The Fairy', a satirical ode to the little lady atop the Yuletide fir. *She is a fairy on a Christmas tree*, sings Florian Schneider, apparently through a cotton wool beard, *See her wave her little wand at me*. The whole nature of Christmas is questioned as Schneider goes on to list all the ornaments on the tree. *A plastic robin and a silver bell/A sort of bugle thing, I just can't tell/A box of strudel, a pen with a nib/A chocolate Jesus in his cardboard crib*.

Then there is the album's magnificent and haunting centrepiece, *Trans-Polar Express*; thirty-five minutes of metallic drum beats, clattering train effects and a sinister programmed voice intoning *Ho. Ho. Ho.* Over a catchy synth riff, the vocals declare, *From Lapland to Helsinki/Full of Airfix and Dinky/A ball for a boy and a little girl's dress/All aboard the Trans-Polar Express*. The effect is at once both Christmassy and sinister, and in bootleg form has been sampled by everyone from Lady Gaga to Stiff Little Fingers.

Finally it's time for the album's classic comedown finale, 'I Wish to Return This Item', in which the band offers a January-chilled keyboard line while – in a melody as melancholy as any in Kraftwerk's back catalogue – Schneider sings: *This jumper is not my size/I don't really enjoy to eat mince pies/I have already six pairs of socks/My cat is frightened of this jack-in-a-box*. As the list of returned presents goes on, it finally dawns on the listener that, for some people, Christmas is simply no fun.

And so it was for Kraftwerk. After they played a tape of the album to David Bowie and Brian Eno, who both said it was 'blooming great', the band decided they hated it, and boiled the tapes for soup. Only a few demos exist, which means there's little or no chance you'll find a copy in your Christmas stocking.

1. We Are the Elves (6.34)

2. The Fairy (3.55)

3. Trans-Polar Express (34.01)

4. I Wish to Return This Item (7.12)

CRITIQUE OF PURE REASON

BY

BLUR

RECORDED: 1995
PRODUCER: DAMON ALBARN
LABEL: UNRELEASED

After the unexpected critical and commercial success of *Parklife*, Damon Albarn felt he had the necessary creative freedom to tackle a project long dear to his heart. Frustrated with the limitations of his songs to date and inspired by his grandfather's example as a conscientious objector and anti-war activist, Albarn set out to reconcile Western and World music and thus bring about world peace. He found an unlikely parallel in the work of Prussian philosopher Immanuel Kant who, similarly, had tried to bridge the gap between the rational and empiricist philosophical traditions.

Kant is famous for his long-winded, convoluted and often nonsensical sentences and yet Albarn found they spoke directly to his heart. Originally conceived of as a purely theoretical project, Albarn stumbled upon Kant's argument that theory must be applied to experience and so, the next day, he booked a recording studio in the lower Westphalia.

Convincing the band to go along with the idea wasn't as hard as he'd feared, especially as they weren't in the room when he told them about it. Much more difficult was sourcing original eighteenth-century instruments – spinets, clavichords, viol da gambas – over which Albarn layered a collage of beats and found sounds, including himself sneezing and snoring. At Albarn's insistence, the sessions were conducted in High German, with catering staff instructed to serve only authentic early eighteenth-century Saxon-Shicklestein cuisine. Reports of Albarn turning up in Prussian court dress complete with ruffle and brocade frockcoat were confirmed when a grainy colour photo appeared on the 'net in 2012 – although rumours that the musicians had to first pass a test on Kant's major works and themes proved to be wide of the mark. In fact, all they had to do was give a lecture on the Copernican revolution and wear two-button polo shirts and horsehair toupees (a look that became known as the Fred Perrywig).

A lovely harpsichord refrain opens the album, then cuts jarringly into a jungle hiss-beat, while Albarn chants *Kant/Kant/Kant* over a hypnotic groove of looped Baboon orgasms. 'Axioms of Intuition' finds Albarn whispering *Mathematical judgements are all synthetical* over delicate arpeggios of Angolan ear flutes, Mongolian horse hooves and a dolphin on backing vocals.

But it is Albarn's brilliant decision to once again bring in Phil Daniels that lifts the album into high gear. The magic that made *Parklife* so successful is rekindled on the supple vocalising of 'Do the Categorical Imperative', with Daniels threatening: *You got to do the categorical imperative/If you don't want to end up a spiv*. Even better is the twenty-three-minute 'Conjectural Beginning of Human History' on which Daniels unleashes his spoken word genius: *I'm going to the track/Or am I?/Is the track even there?/Betting on the dogs/Or are they betting on me?/I don't know/I don't care/It's nice to be free* over a backing track of pygmy chants and Bantu mating calls. The album ends with 'Private Investigations', a glorious take on Dire Straits' ode to Wittgenstein's lesser-known early years compiling a cottaging guide to Vienna.

Sadly, for all Daniels's enthusiasm and menace, his constant mispronunciation of the word Kant resulted in the promo being unplayable on radio. The album was abandoned shortly afterwards and Albarn has never spoken about it publicly. When bass player Alex James was questioned about the recording several years later, he simply nodded knowingly and asked if anyone wanted to buy some cheese.

Britpop historians note how the doomed Kant project directly inspired Blur's greatest rivals, after news of the sessions reached Noel Gallagher. Fired by his intense hatred for the 'pretentious' Albarn, the leader of the UK's foremost Beatles tribute band immediately penned the immortal 'Pleased to Meet Ya' Nietzsche'. Unfortunately, the *Liam on Leibniz* EP never materialised, possibly due to the fact that when Noel suggested the title, Liam replied: 'Fook that. I'm not singing about fookin' biscuits.'

1. Critique of Pure Reason (Overture)

2. The Transcendental Aesthetic
   (Modern Philosophy is Rubbish)

3. Axioms of Intuition (Boys & Girls)

4. Do the Categorical Imperative (... To the End)

5. Metaphysical Deductions (Far Out)

6. Postulates of Empirical Truth (The Debt Collector)

7. Paralogisms of Pure Reason (Interlude)

8. Traüme eines Geistersehers (Bank Holiday)

9. Conjectural Beginning of Human History
   (Vorsprung Durch Techno)

10. A Priory Clinic Blues (This is a Low)

11. Private Investigations
    (Trouble in the Massage Centre)

SORTING OUT
YOUR BIG END

BY

KYLIE MINOGUE

RECORDED: 1987
PRODUCER: STOCK, AITKEN, WATERMAN
LABEL: PWL

The powerhouse trio of songwriters and producers Spock, Aitken, Watermark signed up Kylie Minogue in 1987, but struggled initially to find the right image for the diminutive Australian songstress. After abortive attempts to launch her as a heavy metal artist (*Bring Your Koala to the Parlour*) and a rapper (*Straight Outta Wagga Wagga*) they eventually decided to use the image of Kylie that the British public had already taken to their hearts, capitalising on her popularity as the small screen's favourite female mechanic.

A soap star since the age of eleven, Kylie finally made

the big time in 1986. As feisty Charlene Mitchell, she joined the cast of *Neighbours*, moved in with her mother Madge on Ramsay Street, put on a pair of dungarees and became the grease-monkey most men wanted to change their oil. As her romance with Scott Robinson (played by Jason Donovan) developed, viewers across the UK fell in love with the cheeky grin and oil-spattered overalls of the elfin Antipodean.

Schlock, Aitken, Watermain knew a winner when they saw one.

SAW quickly threw together a collection of mechanic-related synthpop tunes for their new signing to record. Looking back in 1996, Pete Watermelon made it clear that this was a project they had taken very seriously. 'We spent up to twenty minutes on some of those songs,' he told *Railway Enthusiast Monthly*. 'Twenty-five on one of them I seem to remember, though that included having lunch, obviously.' This fiendishly catchy collection of tunes included such disco-driven gems as 'Under the Hood', whose suggestive lyrics are typical of the album's wholesome yet filthy feel: *Let me get a look at your carburettor/Then I might show you what's under my sweater.*

Already sensing the chart-topping fruit that the Kylie and Jason double-act would one day bear, Donovan was brought in to duet on two of the album's most powerful tracks. On the album's catchy opener 'Shall I Pump It Up?' Kylie huskily points out that Jason's rear, off-side tyre is dangerously under pressure, while on the first single, 'Draining Your Tank', the hapless Jason, having put unleaded petrol into a diesel-powered Volkswagen Jetta, begs Kylie to collect the vehicle and tow it to her garage before there is any permanent damage to the fuel pump. The obvious chemistry between the two young stars is clear in every line: *I'll drain it for ya/I'll explain it for ya/If I tell you that I want it/Will you buff up my bonnet?/Yes, and I might even throw in a new diesel particulate filter*.

Of most interest to those revisiting this early work is the video that was made to promote the debut single. With dungaree-clad Kylie wielding her monkey wrench like the sword of Boudicca and Donovan helpless in the face of her sexual advances and mastery of the Haynes Repair Manual, the video has been cited by many as an early feminist porn film. Directed by Baz Luhrmann in a Battersea lock-up, with a perfectly cast Nick Cave guesting as the leering 'Customer With Bodywork Problem', the video is certainly ground-breaking and bootlegs were extremely popular with men who didn't get out much.

It is a tragedy for her millions of fans that Kylie stifled the album's release, deciding that she wanted to stretch herself as an actress, and while SAW went back to the drawing board, Minogue went on to star in works by Ionesco, Brecht and Ray Cooney. More than a quarter of a century after its release however, rumours abound that the Pop Princess is now considering releasing *Big End* and going on tour to promote it. Her management has even hinted that their client is talking about putting those dungarees back on.

We should be so lucky, Kylie!

1. Shall I Pump It Up?

2. Under the Hood

3. Can't Get You Out of My Head Gasket

4. Hot Idle Compensator (feat. Nick Cave)

5. Oil Changes Everything

6. Draining Your Tank

7. Testing the Suspension

8. Body Injection (Thrust Angle Alignment)
   (feat. Michael Hutchence)

9. U Make Me Lose My Bearings

10. My Engine's Flooded (And I Like It)

OFF THE TOP
OF ME HEAD

ELBOW

RECORDED: 2009
PRODUCER: CRAIG POTTER
LABEL: FICTION

After the world-conquering success of their bestselling, award-winning 2008 album, *The Seldom Seen Kid*, everyone suddenly wanted to know about Elbow. The band couldn't go anywhere. It was like Beatlemania for the over-thirty-fives. Their songs were used in adverts and BBC trailers and they were mobbed at airports by tearful, bearded, paunchy men in glasses. Their lyrics were quoted in love poems written by middle managers to young temps to show that they had a sensitive side and weren't just after a quick shag in the third-floor toilets (although admittedly, that would do). In short, they were Alan Yentob's answer to One Direction.

The one question everyone, or at least journalists and TV producers, wanted to know was, how do they do it? What alchemical reactions occur when they're creating an album that makes it so heart-piercingly, soul-wobblingly brilliant? With this in mind, the band made the brave move to not only document the process of making their next album, but to make their next album all about the process of making their next album. At the news, the sound of journalists and TV producers spontaneously orgasming could be heard all over medialand. Alan Yentob made a *lot* of noise.

The band convened at their usual studios in Bury, Lancashire. 'Keeps us grounded, an' that,' said lead singer Guy Garvey. 'Real place, real people. Plus the pub next door does a great line in real ales. None of your twattish fizzy lager 'ere.'

Equipment was set up and the lads got to work, Alan Yentob hovering in the background like a bookish homunculus, daring to ask the questions few would be privileged to. 'Where do you get your ideas from?'

'Oh you know, here an' there.'

'How do you make a record?

'Watch,' said Garvey to camera. 'We'll do it. Craig, play us an open chord on the piano. Lads, join in when you like.'

Craig Potter, erstwhile keyboard player, obliged. The rest of the band joined in when they thought of something to add, mainly playing the same chord on their own instruments. Then Garvey stepped up to the mic.

Now I'll start to sing/The first thing in me head/I'll wring a tune out of it/An' it'll knock yous all dead. Thus was born the title track, 'Off the Top of Me Head'. Yentob, in the background, nodded sagely. Six minutes later, the song was completed.

'Good job, lads,' said Garvey. 'Craig, give us another.'

Potter played another open chord. The rest of the band joined in when they felt like it. *You don't see many dogs round 'ere/Generally, as a rule/But there're ones I can't identify/An' it makes me feel a fool* ...

A look of recognition, of shared commonality, crossed Yentob's face.

Spaniels I know/King Charles, they're the ones with the ears/An' those ones with the funny eyes ... Weimarana/Yeah, that's them/Vimerama./Love that word/Vimerama ... That's the title, I reckon/Vimerama ... Six minutes later, the next song, 'Vimerama', was done. Yentob's smile was beginning to look frozen. He began glancing at his watch.

This practice continued for several songs, including the anthemic sing-along 'Isn't It a Lovely Day' about being happy when it's a lovely day and 'The Clever One', which showed the more poetic side of Garvey's writing, finishing with the lines, *Nick some bits off Philip Larkin/Bob's your uncle/Job's a good 'un*. And another song about cranes.

By five-thirty that day the band were in the pub sampling real ale for real people and Yentob was on his way back to London where he could be overheard on his phone yelling that even Ice T was better than them.

Sensing that the air of mystery around the sacred act of creating an Elbow album was damaged, perhaps fatally, the band refused to release the album and took out a super injunction to stop the release of the documentary. Instead they decided to spend another five years on the multi-million selling follow-up just in case anyone thought that it was all too easy.

1. Some Birds, Starlings, I Reckon,
   Or Maybe Blackbirds

2. Vimerama

3. Off the Top of Me Head

4. The Clever One

5. The Loneliness of the Long-Distance Crane Driver

6. Something Me Dad Once Said

7. You're Bony, You

8. You Sad Bastards

9. Asleep at the Wheel

10. Isn't It a Lovely Day

11. Sithee

12. The Individual Fruit Pie Down the Back of
    Granny's Settee

13. It's a Bit Black Over Bill's Mother's

THE SPICE GIRLS' BOX OF MIRTH

BY

SPICE GIRLS

RECORDED: 1997
PRODUCER: SPICE GIRLS
LABEL: VIRGIN

Kill therefore with the sword of wisdom the doubt born of ignorance that lies in thy heart. Be one in self-harmony. Arise, great warrior, arise
– David Beckham (reading from the *Bhagavad Gita*)

The Spice Girls were on top of the world in 1997. Their first single, 'Wannabe', had become a global phenomenon, selling several billion copies across 345 countries. Their movie, *Spice World*, topped *Sight & Sound's* '100 Best Movies of All-Time' critics' poll. But all was not well at Spice HQ. Late at night, in their hotel-sized dressing room (which was actually a hotel – The Savoy), the girls had begun to feel that awful chill of doubt to which all great artists are prone: were they being taken seriously? They decided to remedy this on their next album, which would be composed entirely of Leonard Cohen covers.

It's a little-known fact that the only thing the five girls had in common was their shared love of Cohen's poetry and song. They had even named themselves after Laughing Len's second book, *The Spice-Box of Earth*. Just to be sure no one would mistake their intent they rechristened themselves – Baby Spice became Dialectic Spice, Posh became Deep Spice, Scary reinvented herself as Zen Spice, Sporty morphed into Meta Spice and Ginger wore a Union Jack turtle-neck.

The initial sessions went extremely well by all accounts, with the Girls introducing their trademark dance routines into songs such as 'Famous Blue Raincoat' and 'Chelsea Hotel #2', creating new layers of meaning heretofore absent in the Cohen originals. The irrepressible Zig-a-Zig-ah refrain in 'Suzanne' is a stroke of pop genius, only topped by David Beckham's spoken word recitation of the 'Gyaana-Karma' chapter of the *Bhagavad Gita* on 'Teachers' – his high-pitched estuary accent breathing new life into the 3,000-year-old words.

Halfway through the sessions Cohen flew in from his mountaintop monastery to duet with Deep Spice on 'Hallelujah', a version many believe is better than the Cohen original and, perhaps even Alexandra Burke's profound reading of this timeless song. David Beckham, knowing of Cohen's well-earned reputation as a ladies' man, stayed very close to his wife throughout Cohen's visit, even at one point fitting her with a two-foot retractable leash.

Tragically, Beckham had reckoned without a Champions League semi-final, second leg away game at Galatasaray ...

The England captain's infamous performance that night – he missed three open goals, two penalties and got sent off after thirty-six minutes for calling the referee a 'bell-end' – now makes total sense given the circumstances. 'My mind wasn't on the game, what can I say?' was all Goldenballs could manage, in an interview for *Match of the Day*, 'I was ... distracted. I certainly got the "hair-dryer" off the Boss afterwards.'

When asked to comment on the sessions, Leonard Cohen peeled a banana, chuckled, and said, 'I do love my spice boxes.'

1. Famous Baby Blue Raincoat

2. Chelsea Harbour Hotel #2

3. Suzanne (Zig-a-Zig-ah)

4. Bird on a Flyer

5. Dance Me to the End of the High Street

6. I'm Your Nan

7. Hallelujah (Old Spice Mix feat. L. Cohen)

8. (I'll Make Sure You) Don't Go Home with Your Hard-On

9. Field Commander Spice

10. First We Take Tiffanys

11. Teachers (feat. excerpts from the *Bhagavad Gita* read by Mr David Beckham)

MYTHS AND LEGENDS OF THE ECONOMIC BENEFITS OF BRITAIN'S ENTRY INTO THE COMMON MARKET – ON ICE

BY

RICK WAKEMAN

RECORDED: 1973
PRODUCER: CAMERON MACKINTOSH
LABEL: BOOTLEG

In 1973, as Britain was poised to join the Common Market, Rick Wakeman was still smarting from the failure of his rock opera, *20,000 Leagues under the Sea*. Staged at the London Aquarium, it had resulted in the drowning of three audience members as well as the electrocution of two dolphins and a shoal of clownfish, thanks to a malfunctioning

Nautilus. So, when nascent theatre impresario Cameron Mackintosh approached him about doing a show based on the Common Market, Wakeman decided to dip his toes into the political waters. And then freeze them.

With Wembley Stadium booked and iced up, Wakeman got to work and immediately ran into problems. Since the show was emblematic of a new Europe, a strict musical quota was introduced and rigorously enforced. Each country had to be represented by a native singer or band. France sent a middle-aged Johnny Halliday, while Italy dispatched its premier prog-rocker, Topo Gigio. There was also a quota on musical notes, with some of Wagner's favourites (E, G and F#) banned due to German sensitivities.

Although firmly committed to the project's integrationist nature, Wakeman could not resist a few of his famous 'Little Englander' digs. Typical is 'The Chateau of Val Duchesse (Sleep Brings Forth Monsters of Progress)' in which he equates the 1956 conference with the infamous Villa Deodati weekend in which Mary Shelley created Frankenstein and John Polidori wrote *The Vampyre*. He is rather less subtle in the jaunty 'Two World Wars and One World Cup', which he envisaged as a smash hit single.

Eschewing his usual cape and pointed hat, Wakeman took to the stage wearing something emblematic of every country. He sported lederhosen, a stripy jumper and a Dutch cap, but suffered a hideous costume malfunction when he got a clog caught in his mellotron pedal.

The show was long, even by Wakeman's standards,

with each country's leader played by a prominent actor from that country, skating round the arena while delivering sections of the Spaak Report. No one who was there could forget Mike Yarwood, TV's favourite 'man of a few faces', as Prime Minister Edward Heath, reinterpreting Wakeman's progressive keyboard runs with his trademark funny voice: *Morning Cloud/That's my yacht, that is/Ooh, hello sailor etc.*

Wakeman, famous for having a curry delivered to him onstage during some of Yes's more otiose and longwinded solos, outdid himself this time. While the show was progressing, he had his chauffeur drive him to the Star of India in Hammersmith where he enjoyed a three-course meal plus poppadums and pickle and a couple of pints of Harp, before being driven back to the gig. His absence wasn't noticed since the show lasted eighteen hours, with each song translated into the native language of every member state.

David Bowie (at his most chameleon-like) made recurrent appearances in a leotard, representing each European country through the medium of mime and interpretive dance. However, during a particularly torturous rendition of 'The Netherlands', Bowie managed to dislocate both his shoulder and kneecap and had to hobble off, bent double, with his head literally between his legs. If one listens closely to the tape, one can clearly hear Rick Wakeman shouting after him, 'That's for my piano riff on "Life on Mars", you fucker.'

The show was not quite as successful as had been initially

hoped, with audience members following Wakeman's example in walking out but, unfortunately, not returning and both the planned tour and studio album were dropped. To this day, Wakeman insists that the failure of the project was solely due to draconian EEC health and safety laws.

1. The European Coal and Steel Community 1951
   (Part One)

2. The Benelux Boys and the Spaak Report

3. The Intergovernmental Conference on the Common
   Market (and Eurotom)

4. The Chateau of Val Duchesse
   (Sleep Brings Forth Monsters of Progress)

5. Two World Wars and One World Cup
   (Doo-Dah, Doo-Dah)

6. The European Coal and Steel Community Revisited
   (Part Two)

7. Don't Mention The War (We're All Friends Now)

COMPLETE AND UTTER COUNTRY

BY

GARTH BROOKS

RECORDED: 1997
PRODUCER: ALLEN REYNOLDS
LABEL: CAPITOL NASHVILLE

On a bright spring day in 1997, after releasing a series of best-selling and profoundly shit albums, Garth Brooks walked into Jack's Tracks recording studios in Nashville and created what has been widely recognised as one of the greatest country records ever made. Brooks was completely amazed, thoroughly baffled, and absolutely horrified.

Producer Allen Reynolds revealed just how terrifying the sessions had been in a 1999 interview with *Cowpoke* magazine. 'It was like the Goddam' *Exorcist* or something,' he told them. 'We'd been all set to make another classic Garth record, you know? Like *Ropin' the Wind* or *Fences*. Same old, same old, you hear what I'm sayin'? I'd already booked a table at the Grammy's for Pete's sake ... ' Sadly, the producer's table would be empty that year, the free alcohol allegedly snaffled by Kenny Rogers, who quickly got sloppy and later flashed his arse at a terrified Willie Nelson.

If anything, Reynolds assessment of what Brooks had actually done was understated. This was a collection of songs quite unlike anything Garth had produced before. Cuts that were real and raw, the instrumentation stripped back and Brooks's cracked vocal rising above the guitar and the pedal-steel to speak for the poor, the downtrodden and the disenfranchised. These were songs that channelled Hank Williams, Johnny Cash and Merle Haggard. The lyrics would have done Raymond Carver credit, dripping with rage and shame; heartbreakingly tender and profoundly furious at the same time.

'I have no idea what happened,' Brooks later said.

At a loss to explain *Complete and Utter Country*, Brooks retired to his ranch in Owasso, Oklahoma. It was many months before he felt ready to make a statement. When he finally spoke to *Country Corner* (twelve-page feature and cover shot) he was alarmingly frank:

I don't really know ... maybe I was ill, or somethin'. I was on these antibiotics after I accidentally sat on one of my CMA awards, so it might have been that. And I'd fallen off my horse a couple weeks before, landed on my head, and I'd been having these weird dreams ever since. Me and Johnny Cash was lookin' down from a mountain and the sea was raging and he was talking about the four horsemen of the Apocalypse. We was both naked, did I mention that ... ? Anyway, whatever the hell happened in that studio, I'm profoundly sorry. That's about all I can say. I'm *so* sorry ...

Once the album had been completed, a sampler was sent out to a select group of Brooks's biggest fans, as well as to several influential journalists. While the journos were amazed and delighted, the reaction from the fans was predictably angry. Brooks began receiving hate mail and abusive phone messages. An old lady with cotton-candy hair and a rhinestone-studded shirt drove out to the Oklahoma ranch in her electric wheelchair and took a shit on Brooks's porch.

Complete and Utter Country was shelved immediately.

Never an artist to disappoint his fans, Brooks called up Allen Reynolds, went straight back into the studio and banged out an album that went double-platinum within a week and yielded the hit single 'The Same Old Shit'.

'It was good to have him back,' Reynolds said.

1. Such a Country

2. What a Country

3. Massive Country

4. Total Country

5. You'll Always Be a Country

6. Country of the Highest Order

7. That's What I Call a Country

8. Big Ugly Country

9. Star-Spangled Country

10. Old Shep's Country

MESSIAH COMPLEX

BY

MICHAEL JACKSON
& MADONNA

RECORDED: 1988
PRODUCER: QUINCY JONES/STEPHEN BRAY
LABEL: EPIC

When word leaked out in 1988 that Madonna had approached Michael Jackson to talk about a collaboration, the music industry held its breath, crossed its fingers and prepared for a sales bonanza. A joint album from the undisputed King and Queen of Pop would surely be the musical highpoint of the decade, if not the century, wouldn't it?

Wouldn't it ... ?

Madonna was keen to make an album about faith; to explore the love inherent in all true religions by focusing on the tender and caring relationship between Jesus Christ and Mary Magdalen. Jackson was assured it would be a smash and was persuaded that it might go some way to re-defining his image a little. He had recently announced that he was 'Bad' and was preparing to show people he was 'Dangerous'. It couldn't hurt to add 'Spiritual' to the list. Jackson was already a man of faith, though he had renounced the Jehovah's Witnesses the previous year, growing tired of people's reactions when he turned up on their doorstep. 'It's because I'm famous, isn't it?' he had asked mentor Quincy Jones. 'That's why they scream, isn't it?'

'Sure it is, Mike,' Jones had assured him. 'Sure it is ...'

Madonna and Jackson spent weeks in Neverland honing the concept for the album and stage show, but discussions were often fraught. She vetoed Jackson's wish to bring Macauley Culkin on board as 'Young JC' (despite the youngster's apparent liking for 'Jesus Juice') and was dubious about allowing Bubbles the chimp to 'perform' on one track as the Holy Spirit. 'That's not really my vision,' she allegedly told the furious Jackson. Relations between Madge and Wacko Jacko would get a whole lot worse when he found out exactly what her vision was.

Unable to grow a beard for his role, Jackson paid a doctor to grow one for him. While he was waiting for the transplant, Madonna set to work on a set of songs. She had hit paydirt by playing on her sexuality and she certainly did not plan on stopping now. 'Jesus was hot,' she told Oprah Winfrey 'He was buff with a cool beard and Mary couldn't wait to "know" him. You ask me, they were "knowing" each other every five minutes ...'

Jackson was horrified and as word began to filter out,

church groups were quickly up in arms. There was plenty for them to complain about, not least of all the artwork that Madonna had commissioned. It featured Jackson (complete with transplanted bum-fluff) on the cross, with Madonna kneeling before him, preparing to 'take the host' in her own inimitable fashion and Uri Geller as a grinning Centurion, complete with curly spear.

The songs were even racier, particularly the opening track. While Jackson *Whoo*s and *Tee-hee*s in the background, Madonna's breathy vocal makes it very clear that this is not an album that's going to be on the Archbishop of Canterbury's Christmas list. *Turn that water into wine/Come over here/Messiah of mine/For forty nights and forty days/I'll move you in mysterious ways.*

While Jackson's management fought to have the project suppressed, a one-man protest movement gathered steam on the other side of the Atlantic. Cliff Richard had once recorded a controversial album of religious songs himself, but felt compelled to set himself against what he saw as 'dirtying the Lord'. He informed his management that his forthcoming Christmas single would make his position on *Messiah Complex* abundantly clear, but after much soul-searching, Cliff was eventually persuaded that 'Jesus Has No Genitals' would almost certainly not be a Christmas Number One.

1. Cross to Bear (Touch My Ass Remix)

2. These Fingers Can Raise the Dead

3. The Coming of the Lord*

4. Virgin, My Ass!

5. Christ on a Bike

6. If I Were a Carpenter (I'd Make a Bed)

7. Jesus Christ Superstud

8. Immaculate Conception (Do You Have Protection?)

9. Three Times a Night (That's What I Call a Miracle)

* The most controversial track on the album, featuring only three minutes of heavy breathing and a small squeak.

HANOI VERA

BY
VERA LYNN DBE

RECORDED: 1967
PRODUCER: VARIOUS
LABEL: DECCA

1967. The summer of love. Elvis Presley had got married, the world was tuning into *Sgt Pepper*, but Vera Lynn was restless. She had grown tired of WI coffee mornings, jam-judging and bridge. She pined for the days when she had felt indispensable; when her patriotic warblings had been a vital part of the war effort. In short, she wanted to be the 'forces' sweetheart' again. So, she took the somewhat strange decision to fly out to Vietnam and entertain the US troops. But nobody could have foreseen the bizarre ramifications this journey would have almost half a century on.

The GIs took to their visitor immediately. They loved her British accent, her chirpy outlook and the way she became 'one of the boys'; giving advice about venereal disease as the troops wrote poignant letters home or just sat around talking about 'poontang' and smoking what quickly became known as 'Veras'.

Back in Blighty, the album she had recorded to coincide with her trip was ready for release. Lynn had brought in several old chums to help out and the results were spectacular. Larry Adler's harmonica solo on 'White Cliffs' was haunting. Max Bygraves duetted with gusto on several tracks and the mournful clarinet of Mr Acker Bilk made 'Ho Ho Ho' one of the collection's genuine highlights.

But back in 'Nam, things had taken a strange turn. Venturing to the latrines one day, Lynn had been snatched by the Vietcong and word that she had become sympathetic to the enemy's cause quickly escalated into a full-scale rumour that she had 'gone rogue'. Within months, stories emerged from the jungle of an Englishwoman in black pyjamas, pearl necklace and pointy straw hat – a ruthless VC enforcer who forced captured US soldiers to play Russian roulette while she worked on a jigsaw of a Cotswolds cottage and 'We'll Gather Lilacs' blared from tinny speakers mounted on bamboo poles. These shocking stories gained credence a decade later, when an early draft of the screenplay for Francis Ford Coppola's *Apocalypse Now* featured Lynn as the crazed Colonel Kurtz, with Lynda Bellingham slated to play the psychotic Englishwoman; whispering 'the horror' as she nibbled cucumber sandwiches and crocheted a matinee jacket, before strolling out of her hut to butcher a water buffalo.

As far as can be ascertained, 'Vera-San' remains in 'deep country' to this very day. Diplomatic efforts to smoke her out having failed, a series of assorted showbiz colleagues have been sent in regularly over the years in an effort to locate Lynn and convince her that hostilities ceased a long time ago. Harry Secombe made a brave, but ultimately unsuccessful attempt in 1973. Who can forget the scene from *Sweethearts of Darkness* – the documentary about the making of *Apocalypse Now* – in which a crazed Dennis Hopper stares awestruck and wide-eyed at the camera, shouting, 'Secombe! They sent fuckin' *Secombe*, man!' Secombe himself was rather more sanguine about his doomed mission. 'I found her,' the ex-Goon told *Radio Times*, 'but it was hopeless. She just blew a raspberry and told me to fuck off.'

Most recently, in 2013, Welsh opera diva Katherine Jenkins volunteered to try and bring the lost forces sweetheart back from the heart of darkness. Sadly, Miss Jenkins has not been seen since and rumours abound in opera circles that a severed head in a bag was all that was sent back to Cardiff.

For Dame Vera, it would seem, the war will never be over.

1. We're Quite Unlikely to Meet Again

2. Melting Pol-Pot (With soldiers of the US Marine Corps)

3. Ho Ho Ho Chi Minh ...

4. There'll be Mig 21s Over the White Cliffs of Dover

5. Eastbourne on the 4th of July (feat. Max Bygraves)

6. Full Knitted Jacket

7. Black Pyjamas in the Sunset

8. Mantovani Don't Surf

9. Charlie Is My Darling (feat. Max Bygraves)

10. I Love the Smell of Horlicks in the Morning

11. Secombe and Destroy

HELP ME MAKE IT THROUGH THE JOINT

BY

WILLIE NELSON &
SNOOP DOGGY DOGG

YEAR: 2004
PRODUCER: NOBODY CAN REMEMBER
LABEL: ER ...

Over the past eighty-four years Willie Nelson has recorded more than seven hundred albums, collaborated with an amazing nine hundred and eighty-seven other artists, shaved twice, and smoked enough marijuana to deforest an area roughly the size of Canada. Nelson's astonishing productivity is often ascribed to the fact that twenty minutes after he's finished recording an album, he'll turn to the engineer and say, 'Gee, it's about time we made a record, don't ya think?'

Willie has duetted with Hank Williams Jnr, Hank Snow,

Hank Thompson, and many other singers whose first name is Hank (most notably on 1994's rather disappointing, *A Load of Ol' Hank*). He has also occasionally recorded the same album twice, having forgotten he'd recorded it only a month before. There are many lost Willie Nelson albums (some *literally* lost, because he couldn't remember where he'd put them) but by far the most fondly remembered, or rather forgotten, is his 2004 collaboration with Calvin Cordoza Broadus Jr., AKA(47), Snoop Doggy Dogg.

'Hey, did I ever make a rap record?' Willie Nelson asked his poodle, Anthony, one evening while smoking a finely-rolled 'Dolly Parton', a type of joint which features two perfectly rounded bulges near the tip. 'No,' barked Anthony and passed back the joint. Nelson called his manager – once he remembered where the phone was. Unfortunately he dialled the Pizza home delivery number by mistake and by the time he'd got through ordering a triple-decked pepperoni, asparagus, mushroom, ham, anchovy, artichoke, olive, tuna, kumquat, duck and bandana pizza, he'd forgotten why he'd picked up the phone in the first place. But eventually (three years later) the call was made and Rap's notorious bad boy (fresh from Billy Joel's *Compton Sessions*) jetted across the desert on his way to Texas.

After initially going to Boston instead of Austin, Snoop arrived at Willie's ranch with seventeen crates of Compton's finest home-tooled weed and sessions got underway to a flying start. Literally, because once Willie had broken out the infamous 'Hank Williams' – a strain of weed so potent it was certain to kill you before you hit your thirties – Snoop had to be stopped from trying to fly out of the ground-floor window of the studio, shouting, or rather rapping, *I'm free as an eagle/They named me after a beagle*.

After smoking two 'Tysons' (guaranteed to knock you out) and a 'Way Long', Willie and Snoop stumbled back into the studio. The rough rehearsal tapes show the two forgetting how to play a C chord, forgetting the lyrics, forgetting to turn on the mikes, forgetting their names, forgetting which country they were in and forgetting to remember to forget.

Recording sessions were temporarily halted when the Federal Aviation Authority classified the smoke cloud above Willie's studio a 'grade-14 airborne toxic event', and again for a much-needed trip to the local supermarket after they both became inexplicably ravenous. Sadly, when Snoop forgot he was black at a Pflugerville County 7-11, it resulted in a potentially ugly situation that was only defused by Willie playing an impromptu version of 'Ebony & Ivory'. This did not make anyone spontaneously hug their 'brother', but did make them direct their hatred towards Willie instead.

The tapes of the final sessions are lost in mists of marijuana smoke. Some critics argue that there *are* no master tapes, that Willie and Snoop actually forgot to record the album. Others claim that on the way to the mastering session Willie and Snoop left the tapes at KFC, where they were battered and fried and then served to a mother of three.

1. Funny How Time Slips Away (When You're Stoned)

2. Help Me Make It Through the Joint

3. Always on My Mind (What is?)

4. To All the Spliffs I've Smoked Before

5. Forgetting You Was Easy > I've Forgotten More About Her ... > If I Could Only Remember My Name

6. (Very) Highwayman

7. Red-Headed Muthafucka

8. Who Am I? (What's My Name? ... Where Am I? ... Who the Fuck Are You?)

9. Can't Remember to Forget You > Don't Forget to Remember Me

10. Three Hanks (A Night)

We Are The Elves

David Bowie at his most chameleon like

Hanoi Vera (holiday in Cambodia not included)

Elbow

BEELZEBUB, BINGO AND BOLLOCKS IN A BUCKET

DOUBLE NIGHTMARE

BY
THE BEATLES

RECORDED: 1980
PRODUCER: GEORGE MARTIN
LABEL: APPLE

The public had been demanding it for a decade. At an estimated cost of twenty-seven million pounds, teams of lawyers had spent years working to make it happen. In the end, it took just one phone call to New York and Paul McCartney asking an old friend a simple question.

'How many fucking loaves can one man bake?'

John Lennon missed the music business. He had grown tired of his life in the Dakota as a stay-at-home dad and (as 'Macca' had guessed) become especially dis-enchanted with baking. His frustration is clear in the snide remarks about baps in his typically Carroll-esque poem 'Yeasterday' and in a comment made to Harry Nilsson that if he ever saw another baguette, he would beat himself to death with it. Lennon was excited by McCartney's proposal. The Beatles' first recordings had been as a backing band to Tony Sheridan in Hamburg. Wouldn't it be fab and gear to do that again? Lennon agreed that it would and so the idea for their comeback was hatched: an album on which the Beatles would back two vocalists with whom they were intimately connected. One side for Yoko and one for Linda.

Double Nightmare was born . . .

The recordings were tricky to say the least. There were never less than seventeen lawyers in the studio at all times, while contractual wranglings meant that there could never be more than three Beatles. This led to some bizarre instrumental choices. Lennon's drumming was iffy to say the least, though it was certainly better than Ringo Starr's guitar playing. Or Ringo Starr's drumming. George Martin has never shied away from the fact that it was a difficult experience, never more so than when recording Ono's vocals, which shattered the glass in the control room on several occasions and, as always, put the listener in mind of cats and mangles. Lacking his usual reticence, George Harrison added, 'She still sounded better than Linda though . . .'

Musically, the album is something of a curate's egg; an egg described by the *Melody Maker* as having 'gone off and smelling like someone has been sick in a tramp's socks'. Yes, Ono's efforts are typically 'difficult' while

Linda McCartney devotes all her time to animal rights, but there are hidden gems. On Linda's opening song, 'Please Please Please Don't Eat Sheep', she bleats repeatedly, as if she *were* one of the poor creatures themselves. It is profoundly moving, despite former bandmate Denny Laine insisting, 'That's her actual voice.'

Of particular interest is the middle-eight in Ono's electrifying track 'Wheeeeeeee'. Some listeners claim that, played backwards, you can clearly hear Yoko intoning *John/Gone* – if these conspiracy theorists are correct, it is a spooky portent of the tragic events a few months later in New York. Though she could just as easily be singing *Jog/On* or *Bon/Bon* or even *Bing/Bong*.

The album looks every bit as strange as it sounds. Unable to decide which of them would design the sleeve, artist Yoko and photographer Linda settled for an uneasy compromise in which Yoko would photograph Linda, while Linda would do a painting of Yoko. Yoko's photograph features a room that Linda has just left, while Linda produced a charcoal drawing of a cowpat, with the words 'Your Face' written above it.

Not particularly 'fab' and certainly not 'gear', but it's the Beatles, so Apple will almost certainly remaster the hell out of it, release it six times in a year in a variety of packages, then put it on iTunes.

Side One (Yoko)

1. Hello, Hello
2. I Like Fruit (Fruit Loves Me)
3. Wheeeeeeee ...
4. Look/See/Wish/Bounce/Gibber
5. The Sideboard Song (Chas & Dave)

Side Two (Linda)

1. Please, Please, Don't Eat Sheep
2. Pigs Are Really Nice
3. Moo!
4. Old McCartney Had a Farm
5. Mary Did NOT Have a Little Lamb Kebab

ARE YOU READY FOR NEW BRITISH ROMANCE? DURAN DURAN VS SPANDAU BALLET

BY

**DURAN DURAN
& SPANDAU BALLET**

RECORDED: 1981
PRODUCER: MIKE THORNE/STEVE JOLLY
LABEL: VEE-JAY

In early 1981, Spandau Ballet and Duran Duran were the kings of the New Romantic scene. They had swept all rivals before them, from Visage to Classix Nouveaux, from Ultravox to all the other bands with a V or an X in their name, and both bands were flying high in the British and European charts. But across the other side of the pond, aka America, neither Duran nor the Spands meant jack-fanny applesauce to anyone. In fact, in several US states, you could still be shot for looking like Nick Rhodes, while in Alabama the bass player from Japan had been sold to a zoo by accident, as nobody could believe something could look that effeminate and not be a gay monkey.

And so it was that both bands – Duran, the pride of Birmingham, and Spandau, loveable leather-kilted North London geezers who were good to their mums even if they did steal her make-up – found themselves without a US record deal. This was an inconceivable slight to their fans – the teenage Durannies and the Spands' Barmy Army – and in early 1980 the bands' managers met up on neutral ground at Watford Gap Services to thrash out a historic deal that, like the Molotov–Ribbentrop Pact between the Nazis and the Soviets in World War Two, was both top-secret and highly controversial. The plan was simple yet fiendish; in order to convert America to the pork-scratchings disco of Duran and the jellied-eels funk of Spandau, the two groups would join together for one amazing album. It would break them across the pond, but far more importantly, would settle once and for all the question of which band was the best!

There had been rivalries in pop before and there would be again – the Beatles and the Stones, Blur and Oasis, B*Witched and Alien Ant Farm – but nothing has ever compared to the sheer venom and rage, the bile and fury spat, spattered and smeared by the twin rival factions of Durannies and Spandies. New Romantics still shudder at the memory of the Battle of the Batcave in 1981, when DJ Billy Wonka was torn to pieces by Duran fans for playing a pre-release of 'Musclebound'. While Luton teenager Mark Wintergreen was forced to change his name and move to Scotland after Spandau fans marked him for death because he'd written 'Girls on Film' on his pencil case.

All of which made it even more amazing that the two bands set aside their differences for one historic album. It was like the Montagues and the Capulets doing a duet of 'Islands in the Stream' at the karaoke. It was like Man Utd and Man City fans getting naked and doing it on the pitch at Maine Road. It was like Roger Waters and Nookie Bear working together again. It was, in short, a unique moment in pop music history and it is remarkable that it even happened at all. What's less remarkable, though, is that it was rubbish. *Are You Ready?* is truly awful: a dismal collection of sub-Bowie clichés and slap-bass nonsense whose only virtue is that it eventually stops. From Simon Le Bon and Tony Hadley's weird assault on 'It Takes Two' to Nick Rhodes's ill-advised rap on 'Going to the Bull Ring (Going to Do My Brum Thing)', the album is an ill-assorted mishmash of nonsense.

It was quickly decided that the album would make both bands even *less* popular in the US and so it was hastily erased from musical history. However, this did not put an end to the feuding, so to settle the issue of who were the true frilly shirt kings, a tournament was hastily arranged and champions selected. Martin Kemp easily beat Nick Rhodes at slaps, but John Taylor levelled matters after weeing higher up a wall than Tony Hadley. It came down to Simon Le Bon and Gary Kemp insulting one another's mums, but when both burst into tears immediately, the contest was declared a draw.

The New Romantic crown would be shared ...

1. It Takes Two (Simon Le Bon and Tony Hadley)

2. Dressed Like Elks and Eating Whelks
   (Spandau Ballet)

3. Cowleyfornia (Duran Duran)

4. Going to the Bull Ring
   (Going to Do My Brum Thing) (Nick Rhodes)

5. Gertcha Rap (Spandau Ballet)

6. Kipper Tie (Duran Duran)

7. Chant No 73 to Oxford Street (Spandau Ballet)

8. These Boots Compacts Are Made For Walking
   (Duran Duran)

CAPTAIN ILLITERATE AND THE TONE-DEAF COWBOY

BY

ELTON JOHN

RECORDED: 1975
PRODUCER: GUS DUDGEON
LABEL: DJM

In 1975, Elton John had it all. With his diamond-studded spectacles, his ruby-studded platform boots and his emerald-studded sapphires, he was the epitome of rock star opulence. He bathed in champagne and towelled himself off with the Mona Lisa. He was superstar excess to the max, and the world was his oyster, or would have been if Tiffany's had made an oyster-prisey thing big enough to open the world. And, in other news, with his song-writing partner Bernie Taupin, Elton's music had won the hearts of millions. Who hadn't ridden on his

'Grey Seal', said 'Goodbye' to his 'Yellow Brick Road', or enjoyed a go on his 'Candle in the Wind'?

But in 1975, Elton was bored. He'd had hit after hit after hit. Even his famous specs addiction was getting dull. Once a notorious specs maniac, Elton was realising there was more to life than specs, gay or straight. Night after night, men and women would find their way backstage and offer Elton unimaginable specs: raw specs, specs with animals on them ... every kind of specs. There must be something else, Elton thought. So he bought some contact lenses and sat down to read Bernie's lyrics. He studied them. Thought about them. And he realised, 'goodness me, these are bollocks. I could do this with my eyes shut.'

At the same time, Bernie Taupin was also feeling a tad hard done by. He'd just bought a piano and was amazed at the way that, when he played it, he could sing words over the notes. He realised Elton John's so-called 'songs' were nothing more than ... well, words sung over notes. 'I could do this,' he thought, 'with my mouth shut.'

Elton called a meeting with Bernie. Bernie called a meeting with Elton. They went to both meetings and agreed: time to swap. Just like in *Freaky Friday* (the original one with Jodie Foster, not the crappy remake with Lindsay Lohan), Elton would write the words and Bernie would write the tunes. They went into the studio with regular producer Gus 'High' Dudgeon, and recorded ten new songs.

The results were unusual, to say the least. To say the

most, they were awful. The problem wasn't that the tunes were bad – although they were *very* bad, or that the words were bad – although they were also very bad. It was the combination of the words and music together. They went together like a horse and carnage. It didn't help that shortly after becoming a piano player, Bernie was shot, but whatever the reasons, *Captain Illiterate and the Tone-Deaf Cowboy* is truly terrible.

It's hard to say which is the worst song on the album, because very few people have got further than the first one. But those who have, and survived, say they can't decide between opener 'My Song' – whose classic Taupin piano riff (which sounds like Les Dawson having his fingers broken) leads into the opening line, *If I was a painter/But maybe not/I'm sorry, what was I saying/I think I've forgot* – or would-have-been first single 'Rocket Salad Man', an ill-advised attempt by Elton to tackle his weight issues head on. Perhaps worst of all is 'Benny Hill and the Jets', a paean to the comedic skills of the much-loved, Southampton-born TV star which features such lyrical car crashes as: *His jokes were sometimes rude/By girls he was pursued/Bespectacled and blubbery/With chicken that was 'rubbery'*.

Unlike Bernie, Elton couldn't write lyrics. Unlike Elton, Bernie couldn't write tunes. And unlike Elton, the album never came out. Bernie spent five years writing speeches for George W. Bush, while Elton disappeared from the charts until the 1980s, when he had a hit with a cover of Salt-n-Pepa's 'Let's Talk About Specs'.

1. My Song

2. Benny Hill and the Jets

3. Someone Shaved My Wife Last Night

4. Honky Donkey

5. Rocket Salad Man

6. Canned Eel in the Wind

7. I'm Still Standing Still

8. Floccinaucinihilipilification Seems to Be the Hardest Word

9. Bernie's Theme (Chopsticks)

DUCK, JAM, LEEK

BY

PATTI SMITH

RECORDED: 1974
PRODUCER: JOHN CALE
LABEL: ARISTA

It takes an artist with the soul of a true poet to watch a tractor trundling past a display of homemade chutney and think that she's witnessing a unique piece of performance art. Thus it was for Patti Smith. On a trip to the UK with then boyfriend Allen Lanier of Blue Oyster Cult, the Androgynous One took a wrong turning off the M40 and found herself at the Brimscombe and Thrupp Village Fete. She stood, awestruck and open-mouthed at the dog show, gawped in wonder at the display of homemade preserves and, after watching the prizes given out for the largest root vegetable, felt inspired to produce what was intended to be her debut album. It would be a hymn to what she saw as the 'true soul of England' and might also help her become as big as Blondie and stop Debbie Harry being quite so cocky next time they ran into one another at CBGBs. 'Jam is life and jam is death,' Smith told *Rolling Stone* while making the album. She also said many other things during the same interview that nobody quite understood, using an accent she had heard while watching an episode of *Poldark*.

Thinking that Wales was a part of England,* Smith asked the extremely Welsh John Cale of the Velvet Underground to produce, and hired recording facilities in the Cotswolds. The sessions began badly. Cale argued with Smith over her insistence on filling the studio with over-sized veg and bales of hay and things came to a head when Smith threw out several of the musicians he had brought in, telling them, 'We don't like your sort round 'ere . . .'

The songs Smith had written for *Duck, Jam, Leek* were spectacular; angry, desperate, heartbreaking and fuelled by little but scrumpy and damson jam eaten straight from the jar. The opening track – a paean to the majesty of duck-racing – sets the tone; the moody, funereal piano chords giving way to Smith's passionate spoken-word vocal: *Run little duck, run/O speedy mallard/Fleeing the fire/All quackers . . .*

'Couldn't have put it better myself,' said Cale, later on.

The playing is deliberately crude and edgy, anticipating the new wave by several years, but it is Smith's provocative and anarchic lyrics that remain noteworthy. The

* It isn't.

Brimscombe dog show had particularly inspired the punk priestess and the poetry of the central suite of songs channel the French symbolists with coruscating effect: *Doggies, doggies, doggies, doggies/Wanting biscuits/Wanting walkies/Big, little, smooth, hairy/The ones that hump your leg*. Her vocals are equally ferocious on 'Bash the Rat' and few could fail to be moved by the howl of anguish that kicks off what had been slated as the debut single: *In Excelsis Dio/Glorificamus te/Get off my land*.

The album cover, shot by Smith's great friend Robert Mapplethorpe, was every bit as provocative. The mono-chrome photograph features Smith in baggy corduroy trousers, topped off with a smock she had seen the Wurzels wearing on *Top of the Pops*. Mapplethorpe added the skinny black tie which would render the shot iconic, though many have suggested that the photog-rapher seemed rather more interested in the oversized marrow in the foreground.

With mixing almost completed on the album later described by the *NME* as 'a fete worse than death', Smith decided to abandon the entire project (after Cale sug-gested she dye her hair blonde) and concentrate on writing solely about dogs. This too proved foolhardy and Smith changed direction after an incident near her home in New York. She had become convinced that her neigh-bour's French Poodle was the reincarnation of Arthur Rimbaud and when she leaned close to commune with the famous poet, he bit her in the face.

1. Oh What a Beauty (Hymn to a Courgette)

2. Bash the Rat

3. Leek of Unknown Origin

4. Brand-New Combine Harvester

5. Because the Chutney

6. Best in Show
   Part I: Poodles Have the Power
   Part II: Retriever with a Lovely Personality
   Part III: A Pomeranian Called Johnny

7. Tractor Beam

BINGO WIZARD

BY

THE WHO

RECORDED: 1968
PRODUCER: PETE TOWNSEND
LABEL: BOOTLEG ONLY

It was the late Sixties and The Who were restless. It was becoming obvious that despite his fervent hopes, Roger Daltrey wasn't going to die before he got old, and Pete Townsend, tired of being branded spokesman for a Mod Generation, was patiently waiting for Paul Weller to go to big school, form The Jam and assume his mantle. In the meantime Townsend wanted to do something different. Flex some talent muscles he hadn't yet flexed. So, after staying up seven nights straight on purple hearts and watching old Ealing Comedies, he hit upon his grand idea: a rock opera. But what would be the subject? He delved back into his working-class childhood for inspiration. He remembered the one thing that had given him

solace as a boy, that had cut through his sense of isola-
tion, made him feel part of something bigger than himself:
Bingo.

Bingo Wizard charts the harrowing story of Graham,
a young lad who goes to the bingo with his mum every
Thursday. One night he accidentally witnesses her snog
the bingo caller, causing him to miss out on a full house.
The combined trauma leaves him catatonic. But it also
gives him a strange power: he becomes the bingo messiah.

The rest of the band had misgivings, but Townsend, in
a flurry of creative inspiration, rushed ahead with the project. Roger Daltrey would play Graham. Drummer Keith
Moon would portray Graham's Auntie Eileen, who looks
after the boy and subjects him to horrific abuse, taunting
him to answer the questions on *Ask the Family*, even
though he didn't know it was on TV, and depriving him
of biscuits if he got them wrong. Moon would also
appear as drug-addled Cousin Kevin, forcing Graham to
take drugs, which wasn't much of a stretch as it was
exactly what Moon got up to while Townsend was busy
writing.

It has emerged recently that Townsend goes to extreme
lengths to research his projects. For *Bingo Wizard* he
actually went to work as a bingo caller in holiday camps.
Unfortunately he kept getting the sack because at the end
of the night he would smash up all his ball-calling equipment and walk off stage.

Songs written, he approached Ken Russell to make a
rough pilot for the BBC's arts program, *Monitor*. Russell

did, and it would be years before the two spoke again. Townsend was mainly annoyed at Russell's insistence on showing a naked Oliver Reed calling the bingo numbers while a chorus of masturbating nuns sang in the background. However, he grudgingly had to admit that having Tom Jones with an enormous pair of hands singing 'Bingo Wizard' was a stroke of genius. As was casting Irene Handl as the Acidly Tart Queen, a matriarch of the bingo halls with a line of coruscating put-downs.

But Jones's song was undoubtedly the showpiece: *Right back when I was a young 'un/I worked those bingo halls/From Yarmouth down to Margate/I've called 'house' in them all/But I'm really rather worried/About how he has the gall/This blind, deaf and dumb kid/Can't call a single bingo ball.*

And therein lay the main problem with Townsend's rock opera, the one the rest of his band members had tried to alert him to: a deaf, dumb and blind kid can't be a bingo caller.

When he realised this, Townsend was devastated and cancelled the project. Only bootlegs remain. Needing a break he got out his old scooter and went to the coast for the weekend. On returning he had created a rock opera about working-class Mods called *Mockneyphobia*.

The rest was history.

Side One:
1. Overture

Side Two:
1. What About the Balls?
2. Auntie Eileen
3. Cousin Keith (Try Some Mandies)
4. 5.15 (Two Funny-Looking Ladies)

Side Three:
1. Bingo Wizard (feat. Tom Jones)
2. Happy Jackpot
3. Hope I Get a Full House before I Die
4. Acidly Tart Queen (feat. Irene Handl)

Side Four:
1. Graham Can You Hear Me? (No, Because I'm Deaf)
2. I Can't Explain (Because I'm Dumb)
3. I Can See For Miles (No I Can't, I'm Blind)

AMERICAN VII: FROM THE DEPTHS OF THE WELL

BY

JOHNNY CASH

RECORDED: 2002
PRODUCER: RICK RUBIN
LABEL: AMERICAN RECORDINGS

Although nicknamed – somewhat uncharitably – 'From the Bottom of the Barrel', there is little doubt that *From the Depths of the Well* is The Man in Black captured at his most intimate and confessional. Producer Rick Rubin had famously reinvented Cash by going back to basics on the iconic American Recordings albums. Before he left to work the same magic with Roger Whitaker on the album that would become *Whistlin' Up A Storm!*, Rubin spent much of 2002 sleeping in Johnny Cash's basement, pre- pared to get busy with a microphone whenever June announced that Johnny was up and ready to go to work. Rubin knew that these were likely to be the last recordings Cash would ever make, so was keen to capture anything and everything, be it first thing on a bright spring morning or in the middle of a dank, doom-laden Louisiana night.

Some ungenerous critics have pointed to the fact that many of the tracks are little more than incoherent mumbling, with only the occasional snippet of anything approaching melody. But as always, the depth and the darkness of the great man are there for all to hear. Who could fail to enjoy 'Humming on the Landing' or be moved at the way a classic is revisited in 'I Walk the Line (Shower Version)' even if Cash does appear to forget the words after a line or two and start complaining about getting soap in his eyes, before breaking into the jingle from the Shake n' Vac commercial.

Particularly haunting is the suite of songs that Rubin later called 'Barbecue', where the passion for the work and for the meat are evident as Cash first bastes his pork, then lovingly prepares it for cherished friends and family members, while muttering to himself. Perhaps not a classic, but a glorious snapshot of an artist captured in a handful of private and intermittently tuneful moments. One for completists perhaps, but there are hidden gems and 'Down!' and its powerful sequel 'I Said, Down!' would surely find a place on any Cash *Greatest Hits* compilation, chronicling as it does, the great man's relationship with his ageing retriever, Digger; a love affair second only to that between Johnny and June herself, whose unforgettable cameo – 'well, where d'you leave 'em?' – makes track four so unbearably poignant.

For more than a decade since Cash's death, the tapes of these final recordings have remained locked up in Rubin's vault, together with his priceless collection of antique beard wax. Sources close to Rubin suggest that the producer is still wrestling with his conscience, trying to decide if twenty-eight minutes of coughing and hawking ('Morning'), yelping ('Stubbed Toe Blues') and cooking, ('Barbecue I–III') will perhaps tarnish the reputation of one of the greatest artists of his time. We can only hope that he makes the right decision, because Cash fans should not be robbed of the chance to enjoy the last, tender outpourings of his genius.

1. Morning

2. I Walk the Line (Shower/Shake n' Vac Version)

3. Down!

4. Honey You Seen My Damn Keys?

5. Humming on the Landing

6. I Said Down!

7. Humming on the Porch

8. Stubbed Toe Blues

9. Barbecue 1: Basting Commentary

10. Barbecue 2: A Man in an Apron Can Still Be a Man

11. Barbecue 3: 'Who's For Ribs?'

FROWN

BY
THE BEACH BOYS

RECORDED: 1967
PRODUCER: CRYIN' WILSON
LABEL: UNRELEASED

At the start of 1967, Brian Wilson was in a very bad place. Months of work on *Smile* had ended in abject failure. The promise of the 1960s was being betrayed on the streets by reactionary politics and rampant consumerism. Brian's brave attempt to solve world problems through the act of smiling had not worked. Assassinations and Altamont were just around the corner and Wilson saw it coming.

Fuelled by late-night conversations with Charles Manson, Wilson set about writing what many consider his masterpiece. '*Frown* was a reflection on what Brian saw going on around him. It was heavy shit, man. Those were heavy times,' Van Dyke Parks later commented.

The first of many arguments and strops was occasioned by Brian's bizarre decision to rechristen the members: Mike Hate, Hell Jardine, Cryin' Wilson, Menace Wilson and Snarl Wilson. Further strain was caused by Brian's edict, punishable by a severe fine, that no one was allowed to smile or make a remotely humorous remark in the studio. Every morning Brian, dressed as death (complete with black robe and scythe), would read aloud the most gruesome stories from the day's newspapers then force the members to meditate on their own mortality for an hour. Five TVs broadcast Vietnam bulletins which, at the time, featured Vera Lynn's kidnapping and re-emergence as Ho Chi Lynn.

The tense and doomy atmosphere led to fractious relations between the members of the band, with stories of entire days spent mimicking each other's voices or tugging at one another's beards. Every time they harmonised around a single microphone, the Boys would surreptitiously knee each other in the balls (which produced some wonderfully angelic notes on several tracks). But, when Brian insisted on the group singing out of tune, it was the last straw. Mike Love/Hate stormed out of the studio.

The album's centrepiece is undoubtedly the 'Paedos and Villains' suite, a remarkably perspicacious take on the creeping menace of child abuse. It's followed by the brilliant double punch of hymns to spousal abuse, 'Bad to My Baby' and 'Please Hurt My Little Sister'. 'I'm in Terrible Shape' consists only of Brian Wilson (then, a massive eighty-nine stone) panting after taking two steps towards the microphone. 'Do You Like Worms (Eating Your Corpse)?' is one of rock's most profound meditations on what is waiting for us all, while 'The Warmth of the Sun (Gave Me Skin Cancer)' warns against the beach lifestyle and recommends staying indoors.

'Surf's Down' is undoubtedly the album's dark heart with its haunting refrain: *I went to the sea/I saw a young man drown/There was litter all around/God, it made me frown*. The album closes with the immortal 'Bad Vibrations': *I'm picking up bad vibrations/She's giving me palpitations*.

The entire suite was performed only once. Brian was so devastated by the results he stayed in bed for the next seventeen years. Often cited as the most depressing album ever made, *Frown* has since found unexpected use as a motivational tool in Tamil Tigers suicide bomber training camps and as a way of cheering up anyone who's been forced to listen to a Kula Shaker album.

1. Paedos and Villains

2. Do You Like Worms (Eating Your Corpse)?

3. I'm in Terrible Shape

4. The Warmth of the Sun (Will Give You Skin Cancer)

5. Surf's Down

6. Freebasing USA

7. Please Hurt My Little Sister

8. Bad to my Baby

9. Wouldn't it be Horrible

10. Satan Only Knows

11. Bad Vibrations

IDIOMATIC

ALANIS MORISSETTE

RECORDED: 1995
PRODUCER: ALANIS MORISSETTE
LABEL: UNRELEASED

1995. Alanis Morissette was riding high in the charts after the phenomenal success of her smash-hit single 'Ironic', but the singer was downcast. Stung by the savage criticism that everything she'd listed as ironic was, in fact, not ironic at all, Morissette conceived of a suite of songs to redress the balance. In an interview immediately following 'Ironic's climb to the top of the charts, Alanis explained: 'I'd always embraced the fact that every once in a while I'd be the *malapropism* queen.' Unfortunately, she didn't know the meaning of *malapropism* either and it later emerged in a rather confusing interview with *Melody Maker* that there were many other words she was confused about, such as 'dimple', 'vociferous' and 'cat'.

Worse was to come ...

The album starts with a simple acoustic guitar over which Morissette screeches: *If I was a metaphor/And you were a simile/We'd be exactly the same/In our semantic chemistry.* A pounding wall of programmed guitars kicks in at this point as she wails the irresistible chorus line: *You're so metaphorical/When you say you're going to kiss me/And then you kiss me.*

'Hyperbolic' is even more catchy and, sadly, even more wrong. *The sun is hot/The sky is blue/I can sing/And sometimes do/Isn't that hyperbolic? [laughs].*

The use of skiffle instruments lends a lively and surprising touch to 'Tautological' with its daring and controversial take on the gender wars: *You and me/We're a tautology/So different biologically.* There is genius in the supremely catchy 'Split Infinitive' with its refrain of: *I'm going to split this infinitive/There – I've just done it.* On 'Synecdoche' she names all the countries in the world for no reason whatsoever while 'The Dangling Participle' is a master-class in imperfect grammar. The chorus of 'Oxymoronic': *'I'm not an oxymoron/I'm like hot ice/There, you see/I'm not an oxymoron* is an exercise in pop perfection, even if she is only half right. But it is on the nineteen-minute closer that the album really steps up a gear.

'The Pathetic Phallacy' is a sublime acoustic slow burner in 7/26 time on which Morissette blames the landscape for the suppression of women throughout history. Sample lyrics include: *The mountain is hard/It wants to touch me/The river is angry/Like my ex-boyfriend when he realises his new girlfriend won't go down on him at the Rothko Gallery*, and the classic: *I fell off a horse/On a sharp protrusion of rock/You took my virginity/You pathetic phallacy.*

A series of videos was made for each song in which Morissette drove around aimlessly while David Bowie (at his most chameleon-like) performed a series of stunning interpretive miming routines for each trope – his take on 'Synecdoche', using only little finger and thumb, has to be seen to be believed.

Unfortunately, before the album could be released, Morissette was arrested by the grammar police and sentenced to two years' hard labour with the *Oxford Dictionary of English Grammar.*

1. Metaphoric

2. Hyperbolic

3. Tautologic

4. Split Infinitive

5. Oxymoronic

6. Metonymic

7. Onomatopoeic

8. Synecdoche

9. The Pathetic Phallacy

IN THE WILDERNESS

BY

CLIFF RICHARD

RECORDED: 19666
PRODUCER: MR 'MR' DE VILLE
LABEL: SCRATCHMAN RECORDS

'I was at a crossroads when I met my new manager, Mr De Ville,' said Cliff Richard, recently. 'Literally! He whipped out a contract and I signed it there and then. That was it. I was off in an exciting new direction ...'

In the late Sixties, things weren't going so well for the Bachelor Boy. The decade had started off promisingly, with Cliff hailed as the British Elvis Presley, but he'd been overtaken by more radical, innovative artists such as Tommy Steele and Matt Monroe. Disillusionment drove him to Christianity. Now, as the decade drew to a close, he found himself out of sync with the free-loving, psychedelic hippie culture. It was time for Cliff to step up and get creative.

His new album would be recorded at Mr De Ville's

studio, 666 Greymalkin Lane, and would see him reunited with the Shadows, here renamed the Dark Shadows. 'I wanted to do an entire album of Christian songs,' said Cliff. 'Mr De Ville agreed, but he didn't want me to trot out the same old stuff about sunbeams and miracles. He wanted me to use some of the more ... challenging parts of the Bible. I remember him saying that, if necessary, sacrifices would have to be made.'

The sessions started well, Cliff thrilled with the edgy new material written for him by De Ville. 'He was great,' said Sir Cliff. 'Mr De Ville seemed to have all the good tunes. And the studio was full all the time too. Lots of people there. He really found work for idle hands to do.'

But Hank Marvin was having problems. 'He changed my walk,' said the bespectacled guitarist. 'Instead of four steps, he made me take five. I told him it felt like I was doing something wrong, like marking out a ... pentagram or something. I'd seen *The Devil Rides Out*, so I knew what I was talking about. Mr De Ville just winked at me and said, "Hank, you're a star. Walk like a star." So, you know ... that was okay.'

The songs were starting to take shape. They included an early version of Cliff's second-placed Eurovision entry, the jaunty 'Congratulations', here called 'Revelations': *Oh Revelations/And jubilations/The beast shall rise up in the end-times from the mud/His wrath will thrill them/And then he'll kill them/The world will see the streets of Sodom flow with blood.*

Cliff threw himself into the rest of the recordings with

gusto. 'Living Baal' (*Got myself a killin', maimin', angel slayin' Living Baal*) was a particular highlight and became an unexpected hit single. 'You've Got My Number (666)', 'Demon Seed', 'Get Thee Beside Me' and the haunting duet with Olivia Newton John, 'Blood Sacrifice', hint at a newly liberated and more complex artist. They were also damned catchy.

'Some of the songs were just amazing!' Cliff told *The Daily Mail*. 'They unleashed something fierce and primal within me. At one point I got so frustrated with Bruce Welch not being able to play the right chord that I almost nearly swore. I mean I didn't, but it was a fucking close thing.'

Sadly, Cliff's excitement proved premature. The album was poorly received and never reissued, and Cliff was swiftly released from his contract. 'I never saw Mr De Ville after that,' he said. 'I think he ended up managing Bucks Fizz. But he did promise me that those songs would keep me youthful, and he was as good as his word. Well it's that or the tennis. Or the monkey glands. Actually, I'm very proud of that album. I still don't know why the critics didn't get it.' A great many critics have been quick to point out that *they* weren't the ones who didn't get it.

Cliff occasionally performs a few of the songs from *Wilderness*. Who can forget his appearance at a rained-off Wimbledon semi-final, entertaining the bedraggled spectators with a spirited, sing-along of 'Blood Sacrifice'? The rain did indeed stop, only to be replaced by frogs.

Those old songs still have potency.

1. Get Thee beside Me

2. Living Baal

3. Blood Sacrifice/Demon Seed
   (medley feat. Olivia Newton John)

4. You've Got My Number (666)

5. Revelations

6. Devil Woman

7. Torquemada's Chamber (Is Wired for Sound)

8. These Miss You Nights in the Desert

9. The Old Ones

10. Brimstone and Wine

TUMOURS

BY

FLEETWOOD MAC

RECORDED: 1978
PRODUCER: LINDSAY BUCKINGHAM/
RICHARD DASHUT
LABEL: WARNER BROS.

Rumours, Fleetwood Mac's 1977 juggernaut of an album, was made in an atmosphere of emotional breakdown, drug and alcohol excess and the sexual coupling of every member of the band with just about every other member of the band in every possible permutation. And any one, anything else, besides. It was the culmination of the permissive, hedonistic Seventies, an era never to be seen again, and the comedown would hit some bands particularly hard.

Bands like Fleetwood Mac.

Reuniting a year later in the Sausalito studios – where *Rumours* had been spawned – the Mac had to face some particularly harsh home truths about the making of their previous album. Their behaviour had resulted in them all contracting some of the most virulent STDs ever seen, as well as several others hitherto unknown to medical science. But this news didn't deter them; in fact they used it to their advantage. *Rumours* had been a confessional album, charting the breakdown of their relationships. The new album would do the same; this time, dealing with the aftermath.

And what an aftermath. The lyrics of the songs they started work on reflected this. 'Loving Isn't As Much Fun As We'd Initially Thought It Was' summed up the melancholy atmosphere that hung over proceedings. '(This) Second Gland's Huge' charted Lindsay Buckingham's astonished discovery of the extent of his own condition and Christine McVie's 'Oh Daddy, You're About the Only One I Didn't Sleep With' confronts her own dismay at not being able to urinate without screaming.

'Welcome to the Clinic, Stevie' was Stevie Nicks's doomed attempt to cure her own condition using alternative Californian make-a-wish-and-make-it-better therapy, while 'Creams' charted her subsequent failure.

But it was drummer Mick Fleetwood who developed the most extreme case. In a twist of fate that cruelly echoed his appearance with dangling balls between his legs on the *Rumours* album cover, his testicles turned blue and grew to an enormous size. It became so uncomfortable that he couldn't bear to sit behind his drum kit.

'He kept hitting them,' said John McVie, his face

deadly serious. 'He'd go to do a drum roll and end up yelping in pain. Awful. We had to get two big buckets for him to put them into. That's why the drumming on *Tusk* sounds so experimental. He still wasn't better. He had to bang cardboard boxes and things instead.'

Lindsay Buckingham, by this time inspired by New Wave and Punk, actually wanted to rename the band Fleetwood's Sack, but thankfully cooler heads prevailed.

After consuming their own bodyweight in antibiotics, the band were eventually cured and moved on. But the music industry was slow to forget. At the ill-fated Brit Awards of 1989, it wasn't a broken auto cue or the presence of Samantha Fox that caused co-host Mick Fleetwood to perform so abysmally. It was his peers in the audience heckling him. 'Show us your gonads, Mick!' whispered a sniggering Elton John, while a clearly tired and emotional Cliff Richard was seen standing on a table shouting 'I'm 96, and I'm still better than you!' Even David Bowie (at his most chameleon-like) got in on the act, performing a conceptual mime for those on his table concerning rapid growth and eventual reduction. Unfortunately – or fortunately – the television cameras captured none of this.

Reviled in its day for being both too confessional and too rubbish, *Tumours* was quickly deleted and fans actually preferred listening to *Tusk*. Honestly. Yes, I know. That bad.

But the last word should go to John McVie: 'I know people hate the album,' he said in one of his more lucid moments. 'I know we went too far, and all that. But you

know, some of the stuff we were doing ... we actually
invented herpes. You know that, yeah? Can you believe
that? Actually invented herpes. So, you know, if nothing
else ... that's something we did. Something we should be
proud of.'

1. Loving Isn't As Much Fun As We'd Initially Thought It Was

2. (This) Second Gland's Huge

3. Oh Daddy, You're About The Only One I Didn't Sleep With

4. Welcome to the Clinic, Stevie

5. Creams

6. Don't Stop (Using the Ointments)

7. You Make Loving Hurt

8. That's Enough Penicillin for Me

9. Not That Funny (Having an Umbrella Down Your Cock)

10. Never Forget (How Painful This Is)

Patti Smith proudly displays her inspirational marrows

Rick Rubin searches for more lost Cash gems

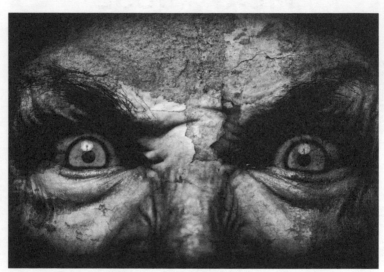

Cliff

MAD DOGS, MEAT ABUSE

AND

MUSICALS IN MACCLESFIELD

GUILTY PLEASURES

BY

JOY DIVISION

RECORDED: 1976
PRODUCER: MARTIN HANNETT
LABEL: UNRELEASED

In the bleak winter of 1975, Ian Curtis was suffering from a debilitating depression. He'd tried every medication available and even spent four weeks pretending to be a dachshund under his behavioural therapist, Dr Schlöng-Schlifenhammer – but nothing was working. Curtis met Peter Hook and Bernard Sumner at a gig in the new year and they talked about putting a band together, but Curtis, deep in the throes of despair, couldn't come up with any songs.

As so often in life, a happy accident changed everything. One night while Curtis was watching a Fassbinder-fest on

BBC2, he sat on his remote control and inadvertently flipped the channel to a screening of *Seven Brides for Seven Brothers* on ITV. Within a few seconds, Curtis found himself experiencing something he'd never felt before – happiness. He smiled for the first time since nursery school and sat riveted to the screen, surprised to find himself singing along.

Ian Curtis became an addict. He travelled down to London every week to see the latest musicals and amassed the greatest extant collection of Broadway bootlegs, including an incredible 445 reel-to-reel set of the complete 1954 *South Pacific* run. He'd never been so happy in his life.

Curtis immediately got in touch with Hook and Sumner and told them he was ready to record. He wanted to name the band Oklahoma, but Hook, obsessed at the time by Lech Walesa's moustache, insisted on Warsaw. Tensions were evident on the first day as Curtis tried to run the band through a version of 'I'm Going to Wash My Nan Right Out of My Hair'. Hook and Sumner's angular backing wasn't gelling with Curtis's sunny optimism but the band knew they would be utter shite without their lead singer and bravely soldiered on.

Curtis was a purist, with a preference for Rogers and Hammerstein or – at a stretch – Lerner and Loewe (he and Hannett famously got into a fist-fight over the latter's predilection for Sondheim), yet somehow reconciling their differences, the band used their punk credentials to brilliantly underscore Ian's flights of joy.

Curtis's version of 'The Lonely Goatherd' from *The*

Sound of Music (sung in the style of Louis Armstrong) is one of the most uplifting and life-affirming tracks ever recorded. His decision to employ a Jamaican accent for 'The Surrey with the Fringe on Top' is a stroke of genius and truly subversive. Ian's well-documented crush on Doris Day yielded his sublime take on 'Que Sera Sera', somehow managing to find hope in this most pessimistic of lyrics. A leaked video from the recording sessions shows Curtis developing his famous dance while trying to copy a Busby Berkeley routine as he croons 'I Whistle a Happy Tune' from *The King and I*.

Unfortunately, on the eve of the album's release, Curtis went to see *Jesus Christ Superstar* and realised that musical theatre was well and truly over. He left in a state of extreme dejection and fell back into a tumultuous depression. Bed-bound for six months, he ruminated on the blasphemy of Lloyd Webber and Rice – a demo of what would become the band's best-known song has him moaning: *Rice/Rice will tear us apart* – the 'us' poignantly being Curtis and the musical – while an early version of 'Atrocity Exhibition' shows that, contrary to popular belief, the title wasn't inspired by the eponymous J. G. Ballard novel but by Curtis's trip to see *Evita**).

From these ashes came the songs that would make Joy Division famous.

---

* Ian Curtis took his own life on 18 May 1980. It is perhaps worth noting that on the same evening, BBC1 screened *Michael Crawford Sings The Best of Andrew Lloyd Webber*.

1. I Could Have Danced (Like an Epileptic)

2. I'm Going to Wash My Nan Right Out of My Hair

3. The Lonely Goatherd of Rusholme

4. Oh What a Beautiful Morning
   (Not in Macclesfield, it isn't)

5. The Surrey with Jah Fringe on Top (Dub)

6. I Whistle a Happy Tune

7. Que Sera Sera

8. Blow High, Blow Low

9. I'm in Love with a Wonderful Guy (... And he's
   called Werner Herzog)

10. So Long, Farewell, Auf Wiedersehen, Goodbye
    (I've Had Enough)

FOUR

BY

REM

RECORDED: 1997
PRODUCER: STIPE/BUCK/MILLS/BERRY
LABEL: UNRELEASED

Where do you go next when you have the world by the throat? This was the question the four members of REM found themselves facing after the unprecedented success of *Automatic for the People* and its eighteen singles. Michael Stipe decided the best way to go would be sideways. Long-time admirers of Kiss, REM elected to copy the band's 1978 strategy of releasing four solo albums simultaneously in order to ease the escalating tensions within the band.

Stipe's original idea was that the albums, when placed side by side, would form the word 'REM'. The fact there were four members of the band didn't dampen Stipe's enthusiasm nor his conceptual creativity and Bill Berry's effort was simply named '.'

Stipe's album, subtitled *Breath*, was the most eagerly anticipated. It was the result of his deep immersion in Professor Houndsnatch's seminal Shleswig–Mittelgrupper theory – the belief that words hinder true communication and that the simple act of respiration is the only true and natural language. Despite the professor being arrested in 1985 on heavy-breathing charges, Stipe became obsessed and vowed to put these theories to music.

During the sessions, Stipe only communicated through breath, which may go some way to explaining why the session musicians sound as if they're playing in different keys (and even, sometimes, as if they're in different rooms). Roping in a selection of famous friends – Natalie Trenchant, KRS-Two, U–Kahnt, and Patti 'Pomeranian' Smith, as well as copious supplies of Listerine – Stipe produced a totally wordless album, yet one which says more about the state of the world and pressing environmental issues than most literary novels.

The album's lead single, 'Heavy Breathing', does exactly what it says on the tin – the blending of Stipe and Trenchant's breath exposing so much about the frailty of human existence as well as the health benefits of Tofu couscous. 'Losing My Breath' had Stipe recording his vocals after running the New York Marathon and is a poignant meditation on ageing, highlighted by Stipe's amazing 32-bar wheeze solo. By this point Stipe hadn't slept for six years, which gave his breath a layered, eerie texture, perfectly suited to conveying the profound message of the songs. Sadly, Patti Smith's contribution to 'It's the End of my Breath (and I Feel Fine)' and 'Exhaling McCarthy' had to be erased due to her insistence on panting like a dog.

Peter Buck went another route. Using the same attention to detail he would later put into The Baseball Project, he recorded *The Stamp Project*, an album about the hidden delights of stamp-collecting. Despite Stipe's insistence that philately would get Buck nowhere, the guitarist went ahead with songs such as 'Columbus Stockbook Blues' and 'Inverted Jenny', featuring his trademark wall of ringing Rickenbackers and soaring choruses. 'What's the Currency, Kenneth?' and 'Tongs & Hitches' further document this most fascinating of pastimes. 'Lick on Me' is deeply sensual despite being about a commemorative Queen Mother first edition set, while 'Everybody Posts' conjures up an aching nostalgia for the days before email. The album ends with 'It's the End of My Limited Edition Run (and I Feel Fine)'. Buck's devotion to authenticity meant the album was recorded onto wax cylinder before being transferred to 1800gm micro-sidereal vinyl.

Mike Mills's album of bass solos is perfect for anyone who's ever listened to an REM album and thought 'gee, this would be great if it was just the bass'. But it is drummer Bill Berry's mix of pop, rock and literate songwriting that, contrary to expectations, is an astonishing left field masterpiece – a deep-searching, spiritual song cycle along the lines of Dennis Wilson's *Pacific Ocean Blue* and Van Morrison's *Astral Weeks* or one of those Jamiroquai albums everyone has on at dinner parties.

Once recording was complete, the band found themselves in a tricky position. They knew their quartet of albums was so good that, if released, it would rewrite the rulebook and render rock music as we know it totally irrelevant. In the spirit of comradeship towards their fellow rockers they decided to supress the release of *Four* and all we have are these rough mixes and partial tracklists. Now that REM have split up, we can only hope these tapes see the light of day, if only to hear Buck singing about licking the Queen Mother.

'R'
1. Breath on Me
2. Heavy Breathing
3. It's the End of my Breath (And I Feel Fine)
4. Exhaling McCarthy

'E'
1. Columbus Stockbook Blues
2. What's the Currency, Kenneth?
3. Tongs & Hitches
4. Lick on Me
5. Everybody Posts
6. Inverted Jenny
7. It's the End of My Limited Edition Run (And I Feel Fine)

'M'
1. Bass Solo #1
2. Bass Solo #2
3-10. Bass Solo #3-#10
11. It's the End of My Bass Solo
(And I Don't Feel Fine Because No-one Bothered
to Listen to It the Whole Way Through)

'.'
1-8. Unknown

MAD C***S AND
ENGLISHMEN

BY

MOTÖRHEAD

RECORDED: 1983
PRODUCER: NONE WHATSOEVER
LABEL: UNRELEASED

On tour with Motörhead in America, Lemmy was feeling desperately homesick. He missed the drizzle, a proper cup of tea and his weekly catch-up with *The Archers*. While the rest of the band were busy throwing strippers out of hotel windows and shagging TV sets, Lemmy hung the 'Do Not Disturb' sign on his door, brewed a pöt of Earl Grey and settled back with a copy of the collected P. G. Wodehouse propped up on his lap.

By the time the band returned to England, Lemmy knew a change had to come. It was not a step to be taken lightly. Coming out in those days was a very different proposition than it is now. Reputations could be rüined and careers finished. Rock musicians, and the New Wave of British Heavy Metal in particular, were a notoriously close-minded and conservative set.

Lemmy's hand was forced when an *NME* journalist, accompanying his nan to a WI bake sale in Stow-on-the-Wold, was stunned to see Motörhead's lead singer dressed in fine houndstooth tweeds and a Barboür, awarding first prize to a Bakewell tart and dispensing medical advice to the old dears.

The sübsequent *NME* interview is a now legendary piece of rock journalism. Conducted in the rarefied airs of Claridge's tea room, Lemmy (wearing a Somerset Maugham bürgundy silk robe over leathers, a monocle, and brandishing a rhino-tusk cigarette holder from the lower Rangoon valley) confided over gin and tonics his heretofore secret passion for a lost and vanished England, a land of bucolic country estates, Sunday cricket greens and, most of all, the songs of Nöël Cöwärd. He also finally confirmed the long-held rumour that he'd been fired from Hawkwind for being caught backstage with a well-thumbed copy of *Private Lives*.

Lemmy managed to convince the band that this was the way out of their creative impasse by getting them blind drunk one night on Singapore Slings. After a short tour of the Far East, in which the band pretended to be dapper Edwardians; and a suitably debauched weekend at Raffles, they retreated to Üpper Bürdock studios where Lemmy immediately sat down at the piano and began to sing, his dülcet tones gently caressing the lyrics to 'Countess Mitzi'. Unfortunately, since he'd never played a piano before, the tapes proved unusable.

There is something at once both thrilling and dangerous in hearing the full Motörhead wall of sound on Coward's 'Don't Püt Your Daughter on the Stage, Mrs Worthington', the guitars shrieking like a thousand scolding mothers over Lemmy's höarse pleas. The steamroller attack of 'Philthy' Taylor's drums adds a muscular dynamism to the inventive pairing of Coward's timeless 'It Doesn't Matter How Old You Are' with the 'head's own 'Don't Let Daddy Kiss Me', while the band's rarely heard softer side comes to the före with surprisingly nuanced versions of 'Half-Cäste Woman' and 'The Stately Homes of England'. The one original, 'Crack of Leather on Willöw', starts as a paean to the gentle sport until Lemmy can't resist singing: *Oh I do love the crack of leather on willow/But if Willöw's not available any ol' prostitute will do.*

Lemmy's irrepressible sense of taste can't help but modify other lyrics, such as by inserting an England football chant into his otherwise tender reading of 'Dön't Let's Be Beastly to the Germans'. The album ends on a high note with a glorious remake of Motörhead's classic 'Beer Drinkers & Hell Raisers' retooled as 'Gin Drinkers & Loüche Wasters'.

Recording was wrapped up in ten days and the band were by all accounts extremely excited about their new direction. They booked a fifty-six-date tour but, sadly, only got to perform the album once. Taking the stage at the Frinton Cricket Club in front of hardcore fans, they manfully played their new material for half an hour under a constant shower of piss-filled pint glasses before being escorted off stage by security.

1. Don't Püt Your Daughter on the Stage, Mrs Wörthington (Unless There's a Pole Involved)

2. London Pride (And Other Beers of My Acqüaintance)

3. The Stately Homës of England (We've Trashed Them All)

4. Don't Let's Be Beastly to the Germans (Unless They Beat üs on Penalties) (Again)

5. Crack of Leather on Willow (Oüch)

6. Half-Caste Wöman (You're Twice as Nice to Me)

7. It Doesn't Matter How Old You Are > Don't Let Daddy Kiss Me

8. No Sleep Till Chipping Södbury

9. Gin Drinkers & Loüche Wasters

MEATHITTER

BY

SCOTT WALKER

RECORDED: 2002
PRODUCER: SCOTT WALKER
LABEL: UNRELEASED

While wandering the aisles of his local Aldi one Sunday morning, Scott Walker was overcome by a sudden urge to punch a leg of Parma ham. It proved to be a moment of true epiphany – a fork in the road of rock comparable to the Beatles' move to Hamburg or Ian Curtis's fateful visit to *Jesus Christ Superstar*.

Ever the perfectionist, Walker worked as a butcher's apprentice in Asda for six weeks. He then travelled to Marrakech to learn from the Master Butchers of Joujouka and was spotted stalking Smithfields market at dawn wearing only a bloody apron.

In the weeks leading up to the recording, Walker roamed the streets of Chiswick randomly approaching people and saying: 'I'm awfully sorry to bother you, but my name is Scott Walker. You may know me from such albums as *Scott*, *Scott 2*, *Scott 3* or perhaps even *Scott 4*. The albums where I actually used to sing. I was wondering if it might be at all possible to slap my hand across your terrier's haunch. I really want to hear what it sounds like. I think it might sound like Mugabe, but I need to hear it for myself, I hope you don't mind.'

'I was outside Gregg's when this strange man wearing a baseball cap came up to little Archie and tapped him with a tuning fork,' Mavis Munson of Acton remembered, still traumatised to this day. It was only after Walker's ankles were mauled by a particularly aggressive Bichon Frise in Turnham Green that he made the decision to move from live animals to cold cuts.

Walker rented a warehouse in Perivale and spent seven weeks meticulously arranging different cuts of meat on a specially constructed wire cage, allowing him to instantly recreate the sounds he heard in his head while setting about the meat with a variety of implements.

Meathitting as metaphor for twentieth-century fascism is introduced on the opening track 'Butcher in the City – Pinochet: GGRFK8363^•ª#¡≠CNT (Beef Brisket)', the dull wet sound of Walker slapping his penis on raw brisket chillingly conjuring up images of Santiago stadium and the amputation of Victor Jara's hands. 'Lamb Somoza' features a terrifying percussion loop of Mung beans trickling down a glass staircase while 'Face on Chicken Breast – Tito: WNKR78903∞¶7•ᵃᵃᵃ§#' explores Balkan history through the sensual glissando of Walker's stubble rubbing against a KFC Zinger. In 'High Heels on Pancetta – *Imelda*' he uses 489 different pairs of shoes to recreate the infamous Manila Monsoon Massacre of '76.*

Walker isn't generally known for using special guests but for these sessions he called in Meatloaf. The singer arrived, excited about the possibilities of duetting their operatic voices, to discover that Walker was only interested in hitting him and using the results as a backing track.

The sessions were enlivened by having to cross a picket line of animal activists every morning and by Morrissey's infamous brandishing of the 'Don't Eat Scott Walker's Meat' placard outside Buckingham Palace. The musicians' resolve finally broke when Walker donned a pig's head to sing 'Pol Pot Roast'. As their instruments started to rot, one by one they deserted until only Walker remained, though he too had taken to wearing a gas mask.

Recording finally had to be abandoned altogether when police, responding to a report of a 'funny smell downstairs', closed down the studio for 567 health and safety violations.

'It makes *The Drift* sound like Herman's Hermits,' one of the session musicians later said. It's just a shame the environmental agency had to destroy the master tapes as a potential biohazard, leaving only these rough yet illuminating recordings.

---

* Walker was allegedly thrown out of six branches of *Foot Locker* for smuggling in a sirloin steak and using it to test the acoustical properties of Nike vs. Adidas.

1. Butcher in the City GGRFK8363^·ª#¡≠CNT –
   Pinochet (Beef Brisket/Vera Lynn's *Greatest Hits*)

2. The Seventh Seal Cull – *Hirohito* (Tuna
   Flank/Spatula)

3. Patriot – *Mugabe* (Zebra steak/Cricket Bat)

4. Lamb *Somoza* (Sweetbreads/Runcible spoon[*])

5. Hitting on Meatloaf (interlude)

6. Face on Chicken Breast WNKR78903∞¶7·ªªª§# –
   Tito (Cheeks)

7. See You Don't Bump His Head – *Mobuto*
   (Gazelle testicles/First Edition Of *Bleak House*)

8. High Heels on Pancetta – *Imelda* (Jimmy Choo)

9. *Pol Pot* Roast (The Lips of an Intellectual)

10. Two Weeks Since You've Gone Off (Adagio for
    Dennis Nilsen)

11. I Slapped a Shih-Tzu in the Streets of Southfields –
    Ho Chi Minh (Dog Collar)

12. The Shoop Shoop Song

[*] No. We don't know either.

CONSPIRACY
OF LOVE

BY
DAVID ICKE
AND TINA TURNER

RECORDED: 1992
PRODUCER: BRYAN ADAMS
LABEL: CAPITOL

After a night in the Groucho Club, during which he had consumed enough cocaine to fell Tony Montana, the head of Tina Turner's management company, Big Hair Inc, had a revolutionary idea. After conquering the charts in the mid-to-late Eighties with hits such as 'Private Dancer' and 'What's Love Got to Do With It', his biggest client was going through something of a fallow period and it was time to do something daring. He told Turner that she needed to team up with a truly controversial figure; someone who could fire things up lyrically and whose input would surely see her back on top of the charts where she belonged.

He had just seen an episode of *Wogan* and knew just the dude.

He then went to bed for a week and forgot all about it.

Aside from knowing that Jim Morrison was the 'Lizard King', David Icke didn't know a fat lot about music, but he was well up for working with Turner. 'She's not from the lower astral dimension,' he said later, 'so we should be all right. She's got a hot body too ... you know, for a woman her age, and I've checked and it's definitely not a holographic veil.' Icke had an ulterior motive, of course. Keen to spread his reassuring message about the Godhead, the global conspiracy of satanic paedophiles and the secret race of reptilians controlling the Earth, he knew that, if he wanted to connect with 'the kids', music would be a useful tool. After meeting Icke for the first time, Turner agreed that 'tool' was the appropriate word, but agreed to go ahead with the sessions because she thought his turquoise tracksuit was quite funky.

Conspiracy of Love is as truly strange a record as you would expect. Turner is in great voice on several of the early tracks, seemingly unaware of just how bizarre some of the lyrics are. Some insist that she had got a little confused and believed she was working on the soundtrack to another *Mad Max* movie. Others suspect that Icke and Tina Turner had grown close and that the former Hereford United goalkeeper and famed loon had begun to influence her thinking. 'I think there's something in that,' an unnamed engineer from the sessions revealed in 2011. 'We were recording out in LA and a gecko ran across the studio floor one day. Just a baby one, you know? Tina went nuts, man ... pointing and screaming. Then she stamped on it with her big glittery boots, shouting, "Take that, Prince Philip ... "'

This seems a little far-fetched, especially considering how quickly things fell apart between Icke and Tina Turner once Icke insisted on sharing vocal duties towards the latter end of the sessions. His reedy, high-pitched warblings on 'Children of the Matrix' are excruciating, but it is the Rex Harrison-like, spoken-word sections of 'Reptoid Hypothesis' that really make the listener reach for knitting needles to plunge through their eardrums.

Turner, though, remains game to the end, bawling soulfully on a reworking of one of her most famous tracks: *River not really deep/Mountain only high because they TELL you it's high/Then they shall peel away their skins/To reveal the scales beneath/For they are truly lizards in human form/Yes, that's what I said, lizards/LIZARDS ...*

The finished album was a car-crash that made Icke's appearance on *Wogan* look like a gentle brushing of wing-mirrors. Despite this, Icke and Tina Turner remain close friends, though the album was, sadly, never released because they could not come up with a catchy name for their new double-act. It was this same lack of imagination that hamstrung the mooted collaboration between MC Hammer and Jimmy Nail.

1. What's the Global Conspiracy Got to Do with It?

2. We Don't Need Another Satanic Paedophile

3. Children of the Matrix

4. Nutcase City Limits

5. Simply the Best (At Being a Lizard)

6. Reptoid Hypothesis

7. River Deep, Mountain High
(Everything You Thought You Knew Was A LIE)

8. Better Be Good to Me ('Cos I'm a Member of the
Babylonian Brotherhood)

NOW, THAT'S WHAT I CALL AN 80s DINNER PARTY

BY

VARIOUS ARTISTS

RECORDED: 1986
PRODUCER: TREVOR HORN/DELIA SMITH
LABEL: SONY/WAITROSE

Arguments persist about which album was actually the first to be released on compact disc (or CD). Some claim that it was Billy Joel's *52nd Street* (about a street) while others insist that it was pipped by Abba's *The Visitors* (about some people visiting some other people). Certainly the first test pressing, at Langenhagen, Germany in 1982, was a recording of Richard Strauss's *Eine Alpensinfonie* (something about muesli.) What is not disputed is that by 1985, the CD had become enormously popular, with Dire Straits' album *Brothers in Arms* being the first to sell a million copies.

Several of the above artists* were also regular fixtures at that most ubiquitous of events on the social scene: the dinner party. As albums slid silently into what were then enormous and expensive CD players, the smooth sounds of Sade, the funky yet non-threatening sounds of Level 42 or the dire sounds of Dire Straits would provide perfect backing music for the serving of chicken Kiev, monkfish skewers or pineapple upside-down cake.

In a unique collaboration between a major label and a posh supermarket, *Now That's What I Call an 80s Dinner Party* (or *NTWICA80sDP*) was commissioned so that diners could now enjoy music that was specifically designed with them in mind. The leading dinner-party-related artists of the day recorded specially written tracks that not only perfectly complemented the food and wine, but also reflected the popular topics of conversation around the IKEA dinner table (See 'Coldplay'). 'Listeners will be catered for in every sense,' said producer Horn, waggling his big glasses like Eric Morecambe. '*Catered* for. You see what I did there?'

As with all such collections, the album is not wholly successful and received decidedly mixed reviews. *Good Food Magazine* declared it 'Somewhat underdone', *Gourmet* thought it 'A bit chewy', while the *NME* simply said, 'As tasty as shit on toast.'

There are some finely prepared morsels for the discerning diner, however. Knopfler's lazy licks and effortless

---

* Not Richard Strauss. He was more popular on the German Techno circuit, where a remixed version of his Violin Concerto in D Minor was popular at Berlin's many S&M clubs.

drawling perfectly suit 'Chatter: With Prosecco' and his lyrics are pitch perfect – *I like what you've done/With the place/Thanks/We knocked through here.* Sade's contribution is typically stylish and slips down as easily as a perfectly prepared Stroganoff, while China Crisis imbue 'I Love What You're Wearing' with just the right amount of turgid triviality: *You look so great/It's just not fair/I could not choose/Which dress to wear/Been changing clothes/All afternoon/Oh this old thing/It's just Monsoon.*

Among the less successful efforts are 'Who's for Cheese?', which makes Curiosity Killed the Cat's previous output sound positively edgy, and 'Arctic Roll, Yum! (No Decent Schools Round Here)' has to go down as a misstep in Nik Kershaw's otherwise faultless career.*

This is nit-picking however, as there is plenty on the menu to enjoy, with the second Straits contribution, 'Table Setting (Boy/Girl/Boy/Girl)' as the pick of the bunch. Perhaps the biggest surprise are those tracks on which artists have rewritten existing classics as part of sponsorship deals with large companies. None are better than Ultravox's Walls-funded reworking of their biggest hit, 'Oh Vienetta'.

Perhaps Horn overreached himself with the inclusion of a hidden classical track from Nigel Kennedy ('A Walk in the Black Forest Gateau'), but whatever the reason, the album proved rather less popular than was hoped and was deleted long before its eat-by date.

* OK, I forgot about the snood.

1. Chatter: With Prosecco (Dire Straits)

2. I Love What You're Wearing (China Crisis)

3. That Starter Was Bloody *Gorgeous* (Level 42)

4. Fish Pie (Whining About Houseprices) (UB40)

5. Trousers Too Tight To Mention
   (Simply Red: Sponsored by Debenhams)

6. Table Setting (Dire Straits)

7. Arctic Roll, Yum! (No Decent Schools Round Here)
   (Nik Kershaw)

8. Who's for Cheese? (Curiosity Killed The Cat)

9. Oh Vienetta (Ultravox: Sponsored by Walls)

10. I Never Thought They'd Go (Chris De Burgh)

FLUID DRUID/
DRUID FLUID/DRUID
DRUID/FLUID FLUID/FLUID
DRUID FLUID/DRUID
FLUID DRUID/CLWYD
DRUID FLUID/DRUID
FLUID CLWYD

BY
JULIAN COPE

RECORDED: 2011
PRODUCER: NONE
LABEL: WHITE LABEL

After a career which had included 1970s indie pop, 1980s stardom, 1990s whocaresdom, as well as books about megalithic Britain, Japanese psychedelia, Krautrock, and a button he found in his mum's purse, it seemed there was nowhere else to go for Julian Cope. He'd tried everything from acid rock to acid-flavoured biscuits, from psychedelia to proto-grunge. He had tried wearing the shell of a giant tortoise after an earlier attempt at testudinal fashion, wearing the shells of two hundred and forty-seven terrapins, had proved unsatisfactory. Then one day, when Cope was writing an article about The Famous Well Knowners – a band so obscure even their own drummer didn't know he'd been in them, he came across a reference to the Greatest Most Lost Album of All Time.

Nothing is known of The Fluid Druids. Nothing at all. We are only aware of their existence because of a photo of John Peel holding their album while his producer John Walters waves a placard reading: 'THIS ALBUM IS REALLY BAD'. Cope had the photo blown up. Then, when he'd glued the pieces back together, he tried to read the track listing with a magnifying glass. What he saw changed his life. A list of the greatest, most obscurely tantalising song titles of all time – but in very small writing and slightly out of focus so he couldn't read any of them.

A lesser fool would have been put off, but not Cope. He decided to rewrite the songs – literally – imagining the titles, the words and the melodies. And, in a studio fashioned from bits of dismantled radios and some seashells, knocked together in the centre of a Neolithic stone circle in Wiltshire, he would rerecord The Fluid Druids' only album. So what if it was a quadruple album where each side had a vaguely similar title? So what if the last two sides appeared to be in Welsh? He was Julian Cope and he could do anything.

Which is precisely what he did. From the rattle-brained opener 'Shamanic Monday', which sounds like Prince playing Twister with the Bangles in a bathyscaphe, to closer, 'Llanfairpwllgwyngyllgogerychwyrndrobwllllantysiliogogogoch of a Thousand Dances', which calls to mind Wilson Pickett being beaten up by a Celtic poet very, very slowly, Cope's re-imagining – or, as many critics said, de-imagining – of *Fluid Druid/Druid Fluid/Druid Druid/Fluid Fluid/Fluid Druid Fluid/Druid Fluid Druid/Clwyd Druid Fluid/Druid Fluid Clwyd* is uniquely appalling. It would be a low point of Gary Barlow's career, never mind Julian Cope's. With its sub-Grand Funk Railroad riffs, annoyingly draggy motorik rhythms ('Amon DULL!' said the *NME*) and its incessant references to standing stones, ley lines and, bizarrely, TV comic Michael McIntyre, *Fluid Druid* ... is unlistenable, in the way that an episode of *Call the Midwife* scripted and acted by human waste is unwatchable.

Days before the release date, every single advance copy was destroyed by Cope in a fit of pique. From time to time, he performs one of the poppier songs from the album, like the gay Stone Age anthem 'Are There Any Real Menhir?' or the album's *Oliver!* pastiche, 'Pagan Fagin'; but so far as music historians are concerned, *Fluid Druid/Druid Fluid/Druid Druid/Fluid Fluid/Fluid Druid Fluid/Druid Fluid Druid/Clwyd Druid Fluid/Druid Fluid Clwyd* remains not just one of the greatest lost albums of all time ... it's two of them.

1. Shamanic Monday
2. Thor Bottom
3. I Still Hate Echo and the Bunnymen
4. Pagan Fagin
5. Three's a Kraut
6. Fluids for Druids
7. The Can Can-Can
8. T-Rex Harrison
9. Are There Any Real Menhir?
10. Druids on Fluids
11. Ley Lady Ley
12. Is This the Rhyl Life?
13. Aberystwyth The Beatles
14. Llanfairpwllgwyngyllgogerychwyrndrobwllllant ysiliogogogoch of a Thousand Dances

MUSIC
FOR HORSES

BY

BRIAN ENO

RECORDED: 1978
PRODUCER: BRIAN ENO
LABEL: GG

Brian Eno was no horseman. 'They terrify me,' he told *NME*'s Charles Shergar Murray in 1978. So it was no surprise that, when he was given riding lessons for his thirty-second birthday, he was tossed off by a stallion and had to spend several weeks in bed recovering. Fortunately he was in a stable condition the whole time and could spend his convalescence planning his next move. He decided to embrace his fear of horses and record an ambient tribute to his four-legged foes.

Whether horses like music or not is debatable, but rock critics loved *Music for Horses*. From the opening track

'No Pal O'Mine Oh', with ringingly subtle guitar by Robert E. Quine, to the drama of 'Redrum Kniw', *Music for Horses* combines the irony-laden rock of his earliest work with the dreamy soundscapes of his later, er, work. Echoes of *On Land* occur on the moody 'Shetland', the triumphal 'Weston Super Mare' and the enigmatic 'Dartmoor/Poe/NY'. Eno invents the mash-up on a glumbient remake of Patti Smith's 'Horses', Mike Oldfield's 'On Horseback' and America's 'A Horse with No Name' – retitled 'Horses on Horseback with No Name'. He revisits the rhythmic sound of *Another Green World's* 'Skysaw' with the much bouncier 'Saddlesaw', and even duets with his old pal Robert Wyatt on the classic reworking of a much-loved TV theme: 'Wyatt Horses'.

Side one hints at what might have been, a nosebag of aural delights which combined the world of nature with that of science. *Music for Horses* remains the only album, apart from Phil Collins's *No Talent Required*, to get a five-star review in both *Sounds* and *Horse & Hound*. We say side one, because the few negative reviews that *Music for Horses* received ('Oldies but baldies,' sniffed *The Barber*) made much of the fact that Eno seemed to have run out of horsey themes quite early on; and they certainly have a point. Only side one directly relates to the concept. Side two is composed of two tracks that 'didn't really fit anywhere else'. There's the uncharacteristically optimistic opener 'Champion the Wonder'. 'It's a track which celebrates life's marvels,' Eno told *Music Twat*. 'We all need to celebrate the marvel of life. We need to ... you know ... champion the wonder.' The rest of side two is taken up with Eno's music for what he called 'a bondage wedding'. The moody 'Leather Bridal' is, despite the naysayers, a brilliant remake of 'Venus in Furs', even if Eno, then a heavy smoker, is at times a little hoarse.

Despite encouragement from his friends David Bowie (who compared the album's livelier moments to 'a black Smiths'), David Byrne (who talked enviously of Eno's 'grand, national vision') and David Bellamy (who found some tracks both 'cweepy and cwawly'), Eno never revisited the themes of *Music for Horses*. This is a shame, not least because he then went on to spend far too much time making Coldplay and U2 sound only slightly less awful.

1. No Pal O' Mine Oh

2. Shetland

3. Dartmoor/Poe/NY

4. Horses on Horseback with No Name

5. Weston Super Mare

6. Redrum Kniw

7. Saddlesaw

8. Wyatt Horses

9. Champion the Wonder

10. Leather Bridal

HELLO,
I HATE YOU

BY
THE DOORS
(FEAT. VAN MORRISON)

RECORDED: 1967
PRODUCER: PAUL A. ROTHCHILD
LABEL: ELEKTRA

'We did it because we thought it would cheer Jim up,' said Ray Manzarek in 1995, after failing to win a bet to talk for fifteen minutes without mentioning The Doors. 'Boy, were we wrong ... '

It was 1967 and The Doors were working as the house band at LA's Whisky A Go Go club. Taking their name from an Aldous Huxley book that a friend of drummer John Densmore's had droned on about in tedious detail when he was stoned, they were trying hard to become America's number one mystic visionary rock and roll band. But they were having a problem with their lead singer, Jim Morrison.

Morrison was struggling to be taken seriously as an intellectual, but was just making himself more and more depressed. 'Jim was always carrying a book,' said Manzarek during the same interview in 1995, long after people had wandered away and found something else to do. 'He loved Sidney Sheldon and Arthur Hailey. I think Harold Robbins was his favourite though.' On top of his passion for edgy literature, Morrison had begun experimenting with drugs, and it was during one such session, taking peyote out in the desert, that a particularly chatty coyote told him in a dream that the lead singer of Them was in fact his long-lost cousin.

Them were playing the Whisky at the same time; in fact The Doors had opened for them. Not literally, obviously, but as their support act, and since the lead singer of Them, the Northern Irish singer Van Morrison, had the same surname as Jim, The Doors frontman took that as a sign that the coyote had been telling the truth. Not knowing the difference between Northern and Southern Ireland and thinking that all Irishmen were either cheerfully violent New York cops or cheerfully violent New York alcoholics, the rest of the band thought a recording session with the pair of them would be just the thing to cheer Jim up.

Wrong.

The legendarily grumpy Van Morrison and the legendarily moodily depressive Jim Morrison got on like the exact opposite of a house on fire. In fact if a house could have been flooded with gallons of water and then submerged in the sea and left there to rot in a wet grave for a thousand years while plankton bred in it, it still wouldn't come close. They hated each other. And the songs they worked on reflected the shared antipathy: tracks such as 'Hello, I Hate You' and the particularly virulent 'People Are Strange (Especially that Irish Spudfucker)'. Van Morrison contributed some numbers of his own, including his paean to British institution *Dad's Army*, 'Rave On Clive Dunn' and, in retaliation for some of Jim's lyrics, 'Brown-Eyed Twat'. Jim teased Van on his cover versions of 'Gloria' and 'Madame George', hinting that the songs were autobiographical and suggesting that the Irishman liked to dress in women's clothing. Van retaliated by changing the lyrics of 'Break On Through' to 'Break That Cocksucker's Face' and on several occasions he actually broke it. Jim Morrison famously made an anagram of his name, Mr Mojo Risin. During the sessions for *Hello, I Hate You*, he also made one for Van: Sir Van Moron. The outcome was predictable.

'Yeah,' said Ray Manzarek in 1995, while his remaining audience attempted ritual suicide, 'it was bad-tempered. We even wrote some lines about Van. You know in "Riders Have the Wind", that line, *There's a stain upon the road/Been squashed flat just like a toad?* That's him. That's Van, because he was ... you know ... like a toad. Jim wrote that. He was a poet, man. A fucking poet.' Manzarek then began crying.

The sessions finally ground to a halt when the two

singers came in to the studio and just sat at opposite ends making up limericks about how much they hated each other. The rest of the band knew it was time to call a halt. Jim Morrison later told *Crawdaddy* that everything he knew he had learned from Van. It was the only time Jim was ever known to smile. Despite spending the next four decades releasing and re-releasing everything The Doors ever did ever, the remaining members of the band couldn't bring themselves to let *Hello, I Hate You* see the light of day.

Jim Morrison eventually tired of the music scene and faked his own death in 1971. He then moved to England, working his way through the novels of Barbara Taylor-Bradford and Maeve Binchy, until he eventually opened the first of what would become a successful chain of supermarkets.

Van Morrison went on to make several albums which became popular only with drug-addled journalists before disappearing altogether from the music scene. He has recently re-emerged in drag starring as the titular character in the inexplicably popular BBC sitcom *Mrs Brown's Boys*.

1. Hello, I Hate You

2. Rave On Clive Dunn

3. Riders Have the Wind

4. People Are Strange
   (Especially That Irish Spudfucker)

5. Brown-Eyed Twat

6. Break That Cocksucker's Face

7. (God, I Wish It Was) The End

8. Light My Fire (Under Van)

9. Gloria (You Like Wearing Panties)

10. Madame George (That's You, That Is)

MARLEY & I & I

BY
BOB MARLEY,
JIMI HENDRIX
& KURT COBAIN

RECORDED: 1967/1980/1992
PRODUCER: MACHINE/TOOLS INC.
LABEL: UNRELEASED

One night in his lonely cliff-top mansion, the 'pop impresario'* had an idea that would change the course of popular music. The vision of an ultimate super-group came to him, a group that would take rock and roll beyond the twenty-first century and, much more importantly, accrue him a shitload of money. Once known for his ground-breaking and experimental programming –

---

* He is called this because the authors wish to avoid potential litigation. And because you all know who we're talking about – besides, mentioning his name three times in one place has actually been proven to be an extremely effective way of summoning Satan.

the reality show, *Brits on the Bog*, where the camera bravely recorded ordinary Englanders in moments of turmoil, indecision and agony as they sat on the toilet, and the unforgettable *Pets Can Sing*, the show that gave us the Doo-Wop Gerbils and the Atomic Kittens – the impresario was in dire need of a hit.

The next morning he asked his PA who the three highest-grossing recording artists were. 'Bob Marley, Jimi Hendrix and Kurt Cobain,' the assistant suggested. 'Great,' said the pop impresario. 'We're going to put them together and form the ultimate super-group.' Nervously, the aide pointed out that all three artists were dead. 'Even better,' the impresario said. 'This way we don't have to deal with all their fucking egos and demands and whining.'

How wrong he proved to be.

After heated negotiations with the estates, a lucrative settlement was reached, and work on a single began. Computer engineers set about splicing and editing the original master tapes, taking off some instruments and adding new backing by the resident house band, Keane.

'Hey Jah (Where You Going with That Shotgun in Your Hand?)' was an instant smash. From the barrios of Brasilia to the slums of Senegal, the single sold millions, reaching number one on the billboard charts and staying there for an unprecedented sixty-six weeks. This is what rock music had been desperately waiting for – the raw, startling sound of the future. The ragged clang of Hendrix's famous opening riff gives way to a bouncy syncopated beat and Marley languidly singing, before a

howl of guitar shreds through the speakers and Cobain
screams. Simply told, it was pop genius. Fans from around
the globe, wanting to see these raw and ready talents in
the flesh, clamoured for live shows.

'Why not?' the impresario said. The subsequent tour
has become the stuff of legend. While artists such as
Natalie Cole and Dweezil Zappa have performed against
a video recording of their dead fathers, this was the first
time the now-common deployment of holograms was
used.

George Lucas's lab spent three months preparing the
holograms for their first show at the Hollywood Bowl.
That night, under a pale fingernail moon, the lights went
off and the unmistakable ring of the 'Star-Spangled
Banner' blasted out. Gasps of disbelief were heard across
the Bowl as a young and dapper 'Hendrix' stepped from
the shadows, got down on his knees and proceeded to
play the riff with his teeth. Halfway through the solo, a
pungent cloud of smoke announced 'Marley's' entrance,
stumbling slightly and singing 'I Shot the Sheriff'. The
audience were stunned and no one really noticed when
the 'Cobain' hologram took the stage. The group played
for two hours and got three standing ovations.

But all was not well. The 'Cobain' wouldn't come out
of his transformer. He briefly spluttered to life then gave
up, not having the will to start himself up again. The
'Marley' refused to go anywhere near the 'Cobain', saying
the honky stunk of death. The 'Hendrix' spent all his time
off sucking up as much extra electricity as he could until

he blew his fuses and had to be resuscitated with a defibrillator. As the tour progressed, the holograms started fighting between themselves, playing practical jokes on one another, and trashing their hotel rooms. The 'Cobain's' lights kept getting dimmer and dimmer. The 'Marley' took four to five hours to get started in the morning and the 'Hendrix' finally short-circuited after a particularly rowdy night at the plugs in Cleveland. Many young female members of the audience were electrocuted backstage while 'meeting' their idols and, as the lawsuits piled up, the album was hastily abandoned.

The 'pop impresario', having installed a fully operational cloning and gene-splicing facility at his Majorca mansion, is currently working on a tour featuring Beethoven, Stan Laurel and Jade Goody, as a way of launching his new TV show, *Stiffs Got Talent*.

1-8. Hey Jah (Where You Going with That Shotgun in Your Hand?) (Mixes #1-8)

   9. Smells Like Ganja Haze

10. Buffalo Ladyland-Shaped Box

11. Three Little Lithium Stones from the Sun

IDEA)!
1) BUY SPAM
2) BUY HAMMER
3) MAKE ALBUM

SPAM

JOB DONE

REFORM WALKER BROS?

Scott Walker handwriting

ENO's favourite horse

Shall I put the Dire Straits on, love?

He's lost control

Index

wanting the angels to wear his
red shoes, 337
Cox, Brian, Prof, 78
Crawdaddy, 26, 75, 88, 103, 319
Critique of Pure Reason, 256–8
Curtis, Ian
debilitating depression, 134
love of Rodgers &
Hammerstein, 134
ridiculous Jamaican accent,
135
contempt for Andrew Lloyd
Webber, 137
Cyrus, Billy Ray, 35

Daltrey, Roger
farming trout, 180
having lovely hair, 178
ill-fated portrayal of Graham
in *Bingo Wizard*, 16–18
Daniels, Phil, 208–9
De Burgh, Chris, 228
and his 'Lady in Red', 229
and 'Lady in Red' as
euphemism, 230
Deacon, John
on being misidentified as Joey
Deacon, 87
on being the only real talent in
Queen, 85
only joking, 86
Densmore, John 126
being dense, 127
Dire Straits
earning money for nothing,
46–239
going down nicely with
starters, 67
music to chat by, 75–7
Dixon, Willie
similarity to Zeppelin, Led,
78–84
success of chain of electronic
retailers, 78
Dodecahedron, 73–6

'Dogs', 44–6
Dolenz, Micky
picking his nose for fifteen
hours, 106
being in The Monkees and
actually *looking* like a
monkey, 107
Donovan, Jason, 212–14
relation to the hippy singer
Donovan, 234
Doors, The,
as sole topic of conversation
for Ray Manzarek, 126–9,
206–8, 319, 326, 400–411
closing, 208
opening, 207
Drugs
ask for 'Freaky George',
07798756743
why they don't work, 234
Duck, Jam, Leek, 113
Dudgeon, Gus, 255
Duran, Duran
and love of Bull-Ring, 91–2
and love of cock-ring, 90–99
and make-up and blouses, 94
saving a prayer for the
morning after, 12, 18–25,
107, 233
Dylan, Bob,
going to see Elvis, seeing
Liberace, 237
having a stupid, whiny voice,
236
playing old songs so that
nobody recognises him
anymore, 26, 28, 331–64

Eagles, The
taking drugs, 167–9, 189, 191,
202–4
taking it easy, 167–9
taking the piss, 28, 45–7,
112–16, 187, 196, 201–3
Ekland, Britt, 388

Acknowledgements

The authors are profoundly grateful to the unnamed sound engineers, studio assistants and bemused onlookers who, at great risk to themselves and their families, were happy to share information with us. We wish to thank those who smuggled tapes, acetates, white labels, photographs, underwear and scraps of hand-written lyrics to us and we are indebted to all the former record company executives who were happy to spill the beans. It's heartening to know that so many years of sustained drug abuse and mental illness have not affected their memories at all.

Our deepest thanks must go to the musicians of course. Even the drummers. Without their hopes, aspirations and ambitions – doomed or otherwise – there simply would be no lost albums at all. As the great Samuel Beckett once said: 'Ever tried. Ever failed. No matter. Try Again. Fail again. Fail better.' Wise words, and we are very much hoping to include the album

Beckett recorded with Cilla Black in *Great Lost Albums Volume Two*.

The gracious quotes provided by Mark Ellen and Phill Jupitus were very reasonably priced, for which, many thanks. Stuart Maconie appears by arrangement with The Tupamaros National Liberation Movement of Uruguay (Penrith Branch).

Mark would like to thank Abba (for the music), beer, the makers of Dorito's and the man who put the ram in the ram-a-lama-ding-dong.

Dave would like to thank Amyl Nitrate (wherever he may find her).

Stav would like to thank Snoopy and Lassie.

Martyn would like to thank Sly and the Family Stone (for lettin' him be both a mouse and an elf again), Talking Heads for sending him an angel and Andrew Gold for being a friend.

We would all like to thank our fabulous editor Antonia Hodgson. Not only did she contribute two of the best jokes (in the Fleetwood Mac piece, about testicles) but she also graciously allowed us to include her favourite band.

But then, all our favourite bands are included in this book. We are fans, first and foremost, and the artists whose albums are featured are ones we admire enormously. Each piece begins and ends with respect, wonder and, above all, with love.

Except Mumford & Sons.

BONUS TRACK

GREAT LOST ALBUMS

BY

THE RESIDENTS

RECORDED: 2014
PRODUCER: MR RESIDENT
LABEL: UNRELEASED/UNRECORDED

It should come as no surprise that the strangest and most perplexing lost album ever made would be by that anonymous bunch of musical terrorists, The Residents. Their forty-year career has been variously described as 'Groundbreaking', 'Seminal', 'A load of old cobblers' and 'Warhol on an asparagus high'. Known for only ever being seen with their eyeball-masks on, for deconstructing popular music, and for making hundreds upon hundreds of albums with undecipherable conceptual gags that only they got, The Residents are intimately familiar with the idea of Lost Albums. Their first two albums (or two hundred – even *Wikipedia* can't make up its mind) are – depending on who you want to believe – truly lost, merely rumoured, or outright fabrications. No one even knows if The Residents who make one album are the same Residents who make the next, or indeed if the people behind the masks are the same people who play the music and not the lead singer's aunt and her three diabetic greyhounds.

The Residents are no strangers to wacky rock-star follies either – *The Third Reich 'n' Roll*, their rock opera about Nazism and carrots; *Eskimo*, which consisted solely of the smooth sounds of Eskimo love-making (the sleeve-notes emphasising how good the acoustics inside an igloo were); and their ill-fated (aren't they all?) Biblical epic, *Wormwood*, where the band dressed in ecclesiastical robes and performed in a brightly lit fluorescent cave, each member acting out a different Bible character. A performance in Athens had to be stopped when the audience took the Biblical theme a little too much to heart and pelted the guitarist with a stone. It was perhaps the first ever instance of a rock musician being *literally* stoned on stage at a gig – but weirder and more insane than all these is the Residents' *Great Lost Albums* project.

Recorded entirely to iPad, dense with vocoder bleeps and synthesizer shrieks, the fifty-one tracks comprising *Great Lost Albums* are sixty-second, compressed cover versions of all the albums you've just been reading about. The Residents tackle Dylan and Liberace's *Las Vegas*

Skyline and end up sounding just like The Residents (or that annoying robot from the Smash ad). Their bellicose version of *Mad C***s and Englishmen* is an amazing telescoping of themes and bleeps and ends up sounding, well, just like The Residents. Their spiky takes on Garth Brooks's *Complete and Utter Country* and *Pistols at the Proms* are miniature masterpieces (though they end up sounding just like, you got it, The Residents).

There are surprises though: The Residents perform Rod Stewart's *Always a Dull Moment* in waltz time, lending a sense of purpose to this otherwise meanderingly quotidian album. Making over The Pogues' *Sucking Off Tramps in the Park* as a reggae mash-up is a stroke of pure genius while adding Hard-Trance splutter and hiss to Elton John's *Captain Illiterate and the Tone Dead Cowboy* could well have been a train-wreck yet the band pull it off. They filter Scott Walker's *Meathitter* through a fermented sheep's head and compress *Dodecahedron*'s fourteen hours into sixty seconds by overlaying all the solos on top of one another, creating a veritable Berlin wall of sound. Their decision to render the Duran Duran/Spandau Ballet album solely on tin whistle and jew's harp is odd but ultimately engaging. Johnny Cash has never sounded as hip as he does here, covered in an X-Factor style, nor was the decision to have a goat sing Bono's parts on U2's *The Satanic Choruses* a totally wasted gesture.

But most fascinating and bonkers of all is track twenty-six, 'Great Lost Albums (feat. J. L. Borges on backing vocals)' – a distillation of the entire album in five furious minutes. Appearing as a hidden track in the hinge between side one and side two (and in a locked sidereal groove on the CD), The Residents have taken the already compressed tracks and distilled them even further so that each album is now represented by a six-second montage of itself. It feels like being trapped inside a hurricane – raging shards of noise and splintered chords crashing through your speakers. You catch a bar of Queen singing about specs, Vera Lynn beamed in from 'Nam, Kraftwerk shaking their jingle bells, a chord from Presley's *Repulsion* soundtrack and then, exactly halfway through, there's a whipsaw of white noise that, if you listen very carefully, reveals itself to be a distillation of the distillation which contains a further distillation nestled inside and so on, *ad infinitum* – begging the question: how many Residents can you fit on the head of a pin?

The album was recorded in twenty-six minutes, despite its running time of just under an hour. A few listeners have detected strains of Paganini or Nigel Farage in the dense multi-layered tapestry of sound, while others have claimed that the album doesn't exist, that none of the albums covered within exist, and that it is all one huge conceptual hoax.

Track List:
  See Contents Page ...